When the Lights Went Down
Crime in Wartime

by **Steve Jones**

For Joycey - a girl who knew how to have a good time!

INTRODUCTION

We've all heard the stories about the civilian population during WW2 pulling together, singing patriotic songs in crowded air-raid shelters and accepting the wartime privations in good heart. Indeed many did, but there was a sizable minority who were determined to help themselves rather than their country. German bombers facilitated entry to other people's houses, and under cover of the blackout, looters set out on their gruesome treasure trove.

The strict enforcement of rationing led to a flourishing black market and emergency laws made a whole new range of offences punishable with terms of imprisonment. The prison population increased by 50% between 1938-45.

Beside the crimes of greed, crimes of passion increased. The enforced separation of husband and wife often led to one or other taking a new partner, often with tragic results when an armed soldier arrived home unexpectedly.

Murderers, black-marketeers, prison-officers, prostitutes and prisoners tell us, in their own words, about their war - When the Lights Went Down.

D0543163

First published in 1995 by
Wicked Publications
222, Highbury Road,
Bulwell,
Nottingham NG6 9FE
England.
Tel/Fax: (0115) 9756828
Web: http://hammer.prohosting.com/~wickedb/
Email: wickedbooks@ukonline.co.uk

© **Steve Jones 2000**

ISBN 1-870000-05-6

THIS EXPANDED EDITION WITH 16 EXTRA PAGES
FIRST PUBLISHED IN 2000

By the same author:

LONDON... THE SINISTER SIDE

WICKED LONDON

THROUGH THE KEYHOLE

CAPITAL PUNISHMENTS

IN DARKEST LONDON

NOTTINGHAM... THE SINISTER SIDE

MANCHESTER... THE SINISTER SIDE

BIRMINGHAM... THE SINISTER SIDE

NORTHUMBERLAND AND DURHAM...THE SINISTER SIDE

(see back pages for details)

Typeset and printed in Great Britain by
J. W. Brown (Printers) Limited, Darwin Press
77a Blackheath Road, Greenwich, London SE10 8PD
Telephone: 020 8691 1357

CONTENTS

"DON'T YOU KNOW THERE'S A WAR ON?"

1. In 1940 a woman making notes on the Woolwich ferry was suspected of spying. The police discovered her secrets at the station.

In the Summer of 1940 police were called to arrest a woman behaving suspiciously on the Woolwich ferry. Habitually travelling to and fro on the short journey between North and South London, scribbling furiously into a small note book, the woman was an obvious spy! When interviewed at the local police station the suspect proved to be neither a woman nor a spy: she was a stevedore decked out in women's clothes. The transvestite's top secret notes turned out to be detailed descriptions of his men friends.

With the German army now firmly encamped on French soil, anyone and everyone in Britain was under suspicion as the probability of invasion loomed. New, draconian emergency laws had already been introduced: a whole new range of offences awaited a whole new range of offenders.

The following stories capture the mood of the times.

A foreigner in Kensington was accused of making signals to enemy bombers by smoking a cigar in a curious manner. He would puff particularly hard to ensure a big light and then point it toward the sky. He was arrested and formally charged.

Two French soldiers, drinking particularly heavily in a London pub, were suddenly overwhelmed by a sense of patriotic fervour. "Vive La France" cried one, at the top of his voice.

So as to not alienate the locals, the second Frenchman quickly added: "Vive l'Angleterre". An Englishman joined the display of patriotism by shouting (or so he subsequently stated), "And to Hell with Hitler!" A woman stormed out of the bar and returned a few minutes later with a policeman. Pointing at the vociferous Englishman she accused him of being a Nazi sympathiser as he had loudly proclaimed the words 'Heil Hitler.' His denials were so forceful that he ended up in court for using obscene words and behaviour. He was fined five shillings.

On another occasion a drunk was fined ten shillings for using insulting words and behaviour. When reprimanded by a policeman for singing loudly in the streets, he was arrested for making the following comment:

"If this is what we pay rates and taxes for then it's high time Hitler was here!"

If anything the police were over-zealous and had too many 'jobsworths' amongst them. They were openly criticised by press and public alike. The Tatler wrote in September 1940:

"While nations clash in mortal combat and the whole earth reels under the flame and blood of cosmic conflict, the London police go quietly and conscientiously about their duties of running people in whose dogs cause a 'nuisance' on the pavement and of making quite sure that all night clubs are conducted on strictly Sunday School lines or else shut down."

An ARP (Air Raid Precautions) worker was stopped by a policeman in the middle of an air raid. With fires raging all around, the bobby began to lecture the volunteer about the severity of his offence. The verbal dressing-down was interrupted with both men falling to the ground as a bomb landed nearby. Brushing themselves down the dogged policeman continued his tirade. The young man's offence? He was riding his bike without a light.

Odette Lesley also found the police officious:

"I came home one night to the flat where I lived in Hampstead and found that the police had broken in. They started to interrogate me in an awful sort of way, saying things like, 'You're an enemy agent you're a fifth columnist, who's paying you?' And this interrogation seemed to go on for such a long, long time until I realised what had happened. I had left a light on without drawing the black-out curtains and, of course, it was shining out like a beacon across the Heath which to them was a signal to the enemy, because it was thought that this sort of thing was being done by fifth columnists."

Odette managed to convince the police that her actions had been through carelessness and she was later fined £2 at the local magistrate's court. For quite some time afterwards she was shunned by her neighbours who would whisper, "Look, fifth columnist!" behind her back.

Some considered ARP workers as little better than copper's narks and the lowest form of life. One warden, seeing an exposed light in a shop window, drew his pistol and shot it out. In a similar case a policeman saw a light shining on the fourth floor of a house in Harley Street. Shinning up the drainpipe to gain entry and put it out he slipped and fell to his death.

There were literally tens of thousands of convictions for lighting offences, not all of the obvious kind. With the blackout being so rigorously enforced the demand for torch batteries exceeded supply and spivs made a handsome profit selling duds.

2. Piccadilly Circus by moonlight. Thousands of prosecutions were brought for infringement of blackout regulations.

3. Albert Mount, a 16-year-old Nazi sympathiser, set fire to houses to help German bomber pilots find their targets.

CONFESSIONS OF A TEENAGE FASCIST

On a more serious note, the following exhibits were displayed in court on 15th October 1940.

1) A box of Swan Vestas.

2) Two burnt Swan Vestas.

3) 18 weekly instalments of 'Mein Kampf'.

4) A photograph of Hitler in a peaked cap.

5) A peaked cap.

Not the normal contents of a 16-year-old errand boy's bedroom. But then Albert Victor Mount was no ordinary boy. He was a Nazi sympathiser and a danger to all those living near his Edmonton home. The headstrong young man decided the best way he could help the Luftwaffe bombers was to light up the skies of London.

When the air raid sirens sounded, Albert either mounted his bike or stealthily made his way on foot to nearby houses and set them alight as their owners took refuge in their Anderson shelters. He unashamedly gave details of one of his arson attacks:

"At about 10 o'clock on Sunday night I went to 177, Herford Road again. I had to be very careful as I could hear the people talking in their shelter. I climbed over the back fences...I did it as the guns were firing. As the guns banged I crept forward a few paces. The back door was easy to open. When I got in I locked the door behind me. Then I went into the kitchen, and with my matches set fire to the kitchen mat. I then put the tablecloth over the fire. I then went upstairs into the front bedroom and set fire to the four corners of the bed...I then hopped it out of the front door and crept back through the hedge in the front garden so I couldn't be seen."

Later in the statement he sought to justify his actions:

"Each time an air raid was on I started the fires to make a big glow to help the raiding German planes if they were low enough to see it. As a matter of fact I have shone a torch in the air on four or five occasions but I thought that was too risky, as where the torch was, I was, and I might have been caught doing it.

I sympathise with Hitler and I thought I could help by starting fires."

Albert was caught by the police at one of the fires he started. After a search of his home, and discovery of the above-mentioned exhibits, he was sent for trial and ordered to be detained under penal discipline in a Borstal institution for three years.

4. The sign says: 'Have a cup of tea'.

A DODGY TICKER

Not everybody was as keen to fight for King and country as the old newsreels and history books suggest. Jack Brack, or more accurately his dodgy ticker, was now in great demand.

Jack Brack was born with a heart far bigger than it should have been. In the twenty years leading up to the war he had to take great care not to overexert himself and had only taken up occasional work selling fruit and chocolates on the market.

Following a medical examination in 1939 at the Drill Hall in Whipps Cross, Jack was granted an exemption notice excusing him from all military duties because of his heart condition.

When not at the market Jack could always be found playing snooker or billiards. One of his favourite venues was the Carlton Club in Osborne Street, Brick Lane. The club was managed by Maurice Kravis, who, at 23, was three years Jack's senior. The elder man outlined his plan:

"I heard about you being exempted. Would you like to earn some money and try and get me out of the Army?"

When asked what he had to do, Maurice replied:

"Go up for me. Go before the medical board."

A deal was struck. Jack received £20 cash and a cigar. Armed with Maurice's National Registration card and birth certificate, he left the real Maurice anxiously waiting in the car outside Tulse Hill recruitment depot. After being sympathetically examined by five doctors, Brack was given an exemption certificate, in the name of Kravis, and driven back to Osborne Street. Jack had served his purpose and been well rewarded. Maurice had no further use for him:

"Don't let me see you around anymore."

Word travelled through the underworld about the scam and Jack suddenly became very popular, reporting for bogus medicals all over the capital and receiving fees between £20 and £60 for his services. Following a tip-off Jack was arrested and confessed. He was made to serve three years penal discipline in a Borstal institution. It's a long time to brood about lost profits. Brack had squandered all his ill-gotten gains at the bookies.

Kravis and six others were sentenced to two years imprisonment.

5. Osborne Street, Brick Lane, where Kravis spent most of his spare time playing snooker.

THE WAR ON WASTE

New offences under the emergency regulations came before the courts every day. In the summer of 1942, Rose Denyer invoked the magistrate's wrath. Imposing a two month custodial sentence, he berated the Stratford woman:

"I regard this as a most revolting, disgusting and outrageous case."

Rose was convicted of wasting bread, margarine, prunes, biscuits, jam and flour.

Mr. Rowland Thomas K.C. continued his tongue-lashing:

"You look well fed. You are 35 years of age and I am assured there is nothing wrong with you mentally and yet in these days when men are giving their lives on the high seas in order to bring us food, you are wasting enough food to feed many families. It's no good fining you. I should not get the money. The only thing I can do - and I do it without hesitation - is to send you to prison, where you will be fed at the expense of the State, free to yourself and I am sure with no waste."

Giving evidence, the Bethnal Green Food Enforcement Officer stated that Rose's rooms were in a filthy condition. She lived on her own and ate at the works canteen. On the kitchen table he found twenty-five large and thirty-two small loaves. The remains of several loaves had rolled off the heap on the table and been eaten by vermin. On the heap were three partly used four ounce packets of margarine and two partly full jars of jam. Two bags containing mouldy prunes and biscuits were also on the table. In the cupboard were another seventeen loaves of bread which appeared to be several weeks old. None of the food was fit for human consumption. When asked if she had anything to say, Rose agreed that she had wasted bread but alleged that the food officer had 'told a few lies'.

In the quest to eliminate waste the authorities even prosecuted a woman for feeding the birds in Hyde Park.

Essential war workers could be fined for being repeatedly late for work, this deduction being on top of stoppages for clocking on late. Jack Battie just couldn't get out of bed and between 6th and 19th August was late on nine occasions, arriving between 6 minutes and one and a half hours after everybody else. He was fined £5. The fact that he might have spent the previous nights in and out of air raid shelters was not an issue.

One week's rations for one person:

Bacon.

Egg.

Sugar.

Cheese.

Meat.

Tea.

Butter.

Lard on ration book.

Cornflakes - on the points ration book.

Prunes - on the points ration book.

Rice - on the points ration book.

Many minor altercations and scuffles broke out among people queuing anxiously at air raid shelters. Other disputes occurred inside the shelters, largely due to the shortage of space. Some families would insist on taking large amounts of household goods, including bedding and even prams, into the public shelters. This caused inevitable conflict. The situation was worsened by the arrival of drunks straight from the pub, among whom fights and scuffles were almost guaranteed.

FIFTH COLUMNISTS IN DRAG

The effects of bombing or combat were often used in mitigation for some, more bizarre offences. One Saturday night in February 1942, P.C. Holyhead was on normal patrol in Fulham when a woman acting suspiciously attracted his attention. She was approaching men on the main road and when they were just a few feet away unfurling her overcoat to show off her assets. As he approached to investigate the P.C. was probably disappointed that the 'flasher' was in fact a male in female clothing. 30-year-old Ernest Ford wore a woman's scarf around his head and under the coat was dressed in silk stockings, a silk petticoat and knickers. A brassiere was filled with inflated balloons.

Ernest, who had in his possession a parcel with trousers and a pair of flat shoes, agreed to go to the police station. En route he obtained permission to change out of his high heels as they were hurting his feet. As he rose after tying his laces he butted the unsuspecting policeman in the stomach and tried to make good his escape. He had not reckoned with the advanced technology of the times. Despite being winded, P.C. Holyhead filled his lungs and blew into his police whistle. The fleeing Ernest was grabbed by another policeman on patrol.

Charged with importuning, Ernest argued that he had just gone out on the streets for a bit of fun. He knew how to play the old soldier, too: he made much of having been wounded at Dunkirk and of being discharged from the army, medically unfit, having lost the sight in one eye.

Mr. G. Freeborough, defending, stated that Ford had told him he had been reading a great deal about fifth columnists dressed in women's clothing. He decided to see if he could be detected and walked three miles without being challenged. Not surprisingly, the magistrate asked for medical reports, before finally sentencing Ernest to six weeks for importuning on the North End Road.

The following month a 19-year-old lorry driver

7. The Paradise Club, October 1939. A girl felt undressed without her gas mask.

came before the court in South London. When asked what he was doing in a stranger's house in the middle of the night he produced a novel defence. He argued that he had been sleepwalking! He, of course, had no intention of stealing anything from the house and when 'woken' by the air raid siren had realised his mistake and jumped out of the window.

A policeman had tracked him down but, as his army papers had come through, and he was due to join up the following day, he was fined £5 and sent off to serve King and country.

Because of the shortage of housing caused by the bombing, it was often necessary for the homeless to sleep in the corridors of flats on a temporary basis. They would obtain permission and set up beds for the night.

Mary Sawles, a secretary living in Bayswater, strongly objected to anybody sleeping 'promiscuously' on her landing. Emerging from her front door armed with a garden syringe, she sprayed two women with a fluid saying that she objected to vermin.

Denying the charges in court, Mary argued that she was only spraying her flat and some of the spray may have passed through broken panels or the keyhole. She added that as the spray was so expensive she would not have wasted it on people like Mrs. Stanley. Mary was bound over to keep the peace.

UNDER COVER OF THE NIGHT

Not all offences violated emergency laws and those determined on a life of crime took every opportunity to profit from the mass disruption. The criminal mind is very quick to adapt to changing times. Hardened young thugs cashed in on the absence of street lighting. On a dark evening in Wood Green in 1940 three men, wearing black face masks, rushed into an off-licence. "Put your hands up!" they ordered the 43-year-old proprietress, Gwen Wehrmann.

Despite the fact that she was facing the wrong end of a revolver, Gwen picked up a bottle and attempted to strike the masked man. Colin Gray, 18, one of the robbers told police what happened next:

"In the off-licence I spotted two women. One was sitting down and the other standing up. I saw Johnnie point the gun to the woman who was standing up and say: 'It's your dough we want.' The woman smiled and said something like: 'Is this a joke?' As she said that her hand went under the counter and whipped out a bottle of beer and struck at the gun. I think that she either hit the gun or Johnnie's hand. She struck at the gun about four times. I heard a loud report and knew the gun had gone off."

Gwen Wehrmann died at once.

The killers made off in a car but no witnesses could make out the registration number because of the lack of lighting. But that was as far as their good luck went. Being young and particularly callous, the gang spent the rest of the evening in a pub. Their general behaviour, together with the unusual fact of their being in possession of a car, quickly drew police attention. When tracked down, the men admitted to a mini crime-wave, both before and after the shooting. Charged with manslaughter, they were sentenced to prison terms of between eighteen months to three years.

'HOW ARE YOUR KNEES?'

With exhibitionists restricted by the blackout, other perverts were freed to use it to their advantage, particularly those fond of 'bumping' into women. One man, a regular offender, was particularly 'clumsy' in the Balham area. Alerted police decided to set a trap. At 7.45. a.m. on a dark January day, Lillian Jagger was bustled in the street by a middle-aged man. Out of the darkness she heard the words: "How are your knees? I would like to stroke them." But 38-year-old William Moore heard something else: "You're nicked" - or the 1940's equivalent.

In 1944, John Clark habitually visited the wives, girlfriends or mothers of men posted out of London. He would tell the women that their loved ones were coming home on leave but did not have enough money for the train fare. So surprised and pleased were the relations that they handed over the fare, sometimes as much as £5, to the plausible caller. Both John and the cash disappeared and re-union hopes were dashed when the women realised that their loved ones were not even entitled to leave.

8. The blackout and bomb damage caused thousands of deaths on the roads.

A GHOUL'S PARADISE

9. Three minutes after a V1 hit a row of shops in Clapham Junction.

With the shortages caused by wartime conditions, it became second nature for some to scavenge amongst bombed-out buildings to see if anything of value could be saved. Many people engaged in this `salvage work' but if caught would have faced a charge of looting and, if convicted, the prospect of the death penalty.

In reality most sentences lasted approximately six months but looting was so widespread by 1942 that deterrent sentences of up to five years were occasionally imposed. Most offenders were opportunists, others better organised and methodical. By today's standards the cases coming before the courts were petty; the accused were tried for stealing such articles as: one tobacco pouch and one pipe; two pairs of gloves; three pairs of socks; one shirt; one pair of shorts; one bottle of hair oil; four packets of Craven A cigarettes and one stick of shaving soap.

A three month sentence was passed down for the theft of a bread-bin, tea, sugar and other items totalling £3.10s. Despite such severity of sentencing, given the strict rationing of clothes, word quickly spread when dress shops and tailors received direct hits.

Gilbert Rayman was struggling to keep his balance as he cycled along the main road. The cause of the problem was the heavy parcel wrapped in brown paper he was endeavouring to carry home. Following questioning by a suspicious policeman he was arrested and later charged with being in unlawful possession of a lavatory basin. He was fined £5 and told to go about his business.

The magistrates continuously reminded offenders that "stealing belongings of the bombed-out is a horrible offence punishable with death." Few were deterred, however, and nobody was hanged. The Police Review in 1941, recommended flogging and, if that did not work, a taste of the rope. It went on to describe looters as:

"Human ghouls ready to profit from the suffering of their fellow men and women."

Most looters were after money, which might often be found loose or in gas/electricity meters. The biggest offenders were those responsible for dealing with the effects of bombing - the ARP workers. Some saw loot as a reward for the dangerous work they were doing; others argued that the stolen property was no longer of any use

11

10. Kids quickly became streetwise. With fathers away and mothers working long hours the Devil made work.

to its dead owners. The volunteers had to be strictly supervised, being otherwise inclined to secrete about their bodies as much as they could carry. Things got so bad that even dead bodies extracted from the rubble had to be guarded lest opportunists rifle their clothing. Many of the supervisors were in league with their workers and turned a blind eye to minor offences. Some demolition men took up the job with the express intention of seeing what they could find for themselves. John Dietrich was apprehended leaving one site with 29lbs of sultanas. He was imprisoned for six months. In November 1943 Roy Ford, a 17-year-old fitter from Fulham, was spotted by a P.C. stealing tea, cigarettes and money from a Kensington milk bar which had just been bombed. When asked what he was doing he replied:

"Helping myself, the same as you are."

Indeed, about half the cases coming before the courts found ARP volunteers in the dock. Some worked in highly organised gangs taking all the lead from wrecked houses, loading it onto trucks for sale some 100 miles away.

One foreman, disgusted with the thieving ways of his gang, picked up a handbag on a bomb site and took out an empty purse. Turning to his men he remarked:

"It's the funniest bloody bomb I ever came across. I have been all through the last war and I done several jobs in this, but I never came across a bomb like it. It's blown every bag open and knocked the money out; its even knocked the money out of the gas meters, yet it didn't break the electric light bulb in the basement."

Many Londoners took their valuables with them into the shelters, but those who stayed in their homes would stow jewellery, savings certificates and cash in boxes under the bed. Those who survived the bombing were often under double-attack, from the Germans in the air, their fellow countrymen on the ground. The English vultures would move in while families were displaced and still in a state of shock.

Gladys Strelitz, newly parted from her evacuated children, was still choking back the tears when she arrived home to face a fresh crisis:

"We went home to find that all around us was shattered. We had just had our windows blown out, but people had been in and looted my home and all the bed linen and everything was stolen and,

well, we were full of despair. It was sad enough leaving the children, but to come home to that!"

Uniforms were fairly easy to obtain and bogus ARP workers and even firemen arrived on site to see what they could scavenge. Sometimes women would pretend to be bomb victims in order to sift through the remains of 'their' homes.

11. A soldier comforts his mother after their house had been bombed in 1941. Many had their life savings and jewellery stolen.

12. *Salvaging valued possessions. Those who took goods away were not always their owners.*

13. *A small number of ARP workers brought disgrace on the volunteers by helping themselves before they helped the victims of bombing.*

14. Gas and electricity meters were broken open and jewellery and valuables secreted about the person of some of the rescue workers.

Probably the most callous story from the Blitz follows the bombing of an up-market club. Dressed in their finery, some of London's richest residents suffered a direct hit in the Cafe de Paris. In the ensuing pandemonium, whilst some women were having their wounds bathed in champagne, the looters moved in. The emergency services did not arrive until some 45 minutes after the first looters. Glass cases containing jewellery, perfumes and other valuables were rifled. The owner of the club, who died in the blast, had his cuff links stolen. One victim remembers being semi-conscious amongst the dust and rubble. She recalls the pleasure of feeling a warm human hand gripping her fingers. She had been rescued! Her elation quickly turned to despair, however, when her saviour tried to relieve her of her diamond ring.

Another survivor recalled the human ghoul who scoured the debris in search of the seriously injured. Finding such victims, from a distance of some six inches, he spoke into their faces:

"Are you prepared to meet your God?"

A third survivor who staggered from the ruins managed to find a taxi to take him to hospital. After a few minutes drive the taxi-driver turned round to his customer and made a polite request:

"Kindly don't bleed on the seats."

On top of the physical devastation, the bombing led to serious psychological problems

15. *Aftermath of the bombing at the Café de Paris (1941). Ghouls and looters arrived to strip the dead and injured of their valuables.*

WHILE THE BALANCE OF THEIR MINDS WAS DISTURBED

16. Many lost their homes and possessions. Some lost their sanity.

Ida Rodway gave the following statement to Hackney Police on 1st October 1940:

"I want to tell you everything. I have been worried out of my life.

My husband, Joseph William Rodway was 71 years old. We were married on 15th April, 1901. We have always lived happily together. My husband was a cabman but he has been out of work for many years. We lived together at Martello Street, Hackney. My husband went blind in April, 1939, and since then I have had to do everything for him, even to lead him about the house.

I worked as a boot machinist for A&H Meltzers, Pretoria Shoe Works on Pretoria Road, Tottenham, from September 1924 until July 1940, when I was put off owing to slackness of work. My husband *was drawing the old age pension and since July I was getting 26 shillings per week labour money. That was the only money we had to live on. I paid eight shillings and fourpence a week rent for my three rooms. On 21st September we were bombed out of our home at 11, Martello Street. My husband and I were in our Anderson shelter at the time. The ARP people got my husband out of the shelter and took him to Hackney Hospital. I went to stay with some friends at 38, Greenway Avenue, Walthamstow.*

After my husband had been in Hackney Hospital for two or three days the people at the hospital told me there was nothing the matter with him except his blindness and that I would have to take him out of hospital. The lady almoner gave me three days to fetch him out. I was worried having no home and didn't know what to do. I went to my single sister, Miss Florence Clapp, 39, Kingshold Road, and I asked her if we could stay there. She said we could and I brought my husband out of hospital on 28th September. My husband and I slept on the floor in the back room. It was a terrible trouble for me looking after him in a strange house. He did not know where he was in another house and kept thinking he was in his own house. I was getting my labour money but was wondering all the time what I should do when that was stopped and how I could keep both of us on ten shillings a week. There was my home too. I didn't know what I could do with that when they started pulling the house down, or where I could take the furniture. It seemed I had nowhere to go and no one to help me. My sister went to work this morning 1st October at about twenty to eight. I thought to myself:

'What shall I do? Here I am stranded with nowhere to go. Whatever shall I do?'

I knew my sister couldn't keep me there for ever. My husband was in bed on the floor, I had been up since about seven o'clock. I was dressed. I was going to take him in a cup of tea, but I never gave him the tea. I got hold of the chopper from under the dresser in the kitchen and the carving knife. I went into the bedroom and he was sitting up in bed. I hit him on the head with the chopper. The head of the chopper fell off. My husband said:

'Oh what are you doing this for?'

I said: 'I am led to desperation' and got hold of the knife and finished him off. I was worried to death with no one to help me. We had not had a quarrel.

This statement has been read to me and it is true.

(Sgd) Ida Ethel Rodway"
11.10 a.m. 1st October 1940.

Ida calmly told a neighbour that she had murdered her husband and asked for a policeman to be fetched. Following a brief examination of the body, whose head had been covered with two bloodstained pillows, Ida was arrested. Joseph had died as a result of several lacerated wounds to the head and neck caused by a hatchet and carving knife.

From her statement it appears as if Ida acted on impulse and the murder was a result of temporary insanity. The police, however, asked some questions in the neighbourhood and found a knife grinder who testified that he had, at Ida's request, sharpened both the knife and the chopper shortly before the murder.

The medical officer, reporting on Ida after observing her in detention, stated that she told him she thought her actions were right and for the best as she had put her husband out of his misery. He continued his report:

"She sits quietly by her bed, never speaks unless in reply to questions and takes no part whatever in the life of the ward ... She still has definite suicide tendencies."

Ida was tried on 12th November 1940 and found to be insane. She was ordered to be kept in strict custody until His Majesty's pleasure be known.

The bombing, without physically doing the Rodways a great deal of harm, had destroyed two lives. Ida's sister testified that Ida often told her she wished they had both been in the house when the bomb dropped, rather than in the shelter.

Cyril Clarke, a 39-year-old train driver, never got over the death of his daughter in an air raid in February 1944. The whole family of five had been buried in the debris and following the raid Cyril suffered from shock and gastric ulcers. He also convinced himself he had cancer.

He left work and sat in his home brooding for six months before instigating his final solution. After a marriage that had lasted some fifteen years, he battered his wife senseless in the scullery with a rolling pin. He then attached a flexible gas tube to the fire and lay, fully-clothed, on the bed. Covering himself with the eiderdown, he inserted the other end of the tube into his mouth and departed on the long journey in search of his daughter.

When discovered, the couple were just holding on to life but both died, Cyril after prolonged artificial respiration in the ambulance and Florence almost at once. The post-mortem revealed no signs of cancer and nobody contested the verdict that Clarke had murdered his wife and then taken his own life while the balance of his mind was disturbed.

17. A direct hit in suburbia. A dentist gassed himself as he could no longer face his work as an ARP officer, 'picking out bits and pieces of dead bodies' from the ruins.

18. Stepney Way, East London. The bombing led to several cases of murder and suicide by people 'no longer responsible for their actions'.

With mothers being worn out and fathers away there was an increase in the numbers of children suffocating in their cots, choking over food and having fatal accidents in the home. The conditions after the war were almost as stressful. In 1946 a 6-year-old boy begged his servant mother to be allowed to go to school. As she was feeling depressed and needed company she insisted that he stay at home. The headstrong boy was having none of this and in the struggle that followed he laddered his mother's stocking. The mother thereupon strangled the boy with a green scarf.

Quite why John Patrick Hopkins put his head in the gas oven will probably never be known, though in June, 1946, the Poplar coroner tentatively put forward this theory:

"One supposes that having been in the Army he did miss his friends. He was an introspective type, fond of reading and undoubtedly he was a bit depressed."

The 41-year-old bachelor committed suicide just five weeks after being demobbed. Beside the body lay a detailed map showing the movements and activities of his unit from D-Day onwards with extracts from a poem written on the back:

*"Can death be solved when life is
    but a dream,
And sense of bliss pass as a
    phantom by
The transient pleasures as a vision
    seem
And yet we think the greatest
    pain's to die."*

There were no suspicious circumstances and the coroner recorded a verdict of 'suicide while the balance of his mind was disturbed'.

John Stone was a workaholic. With his wife and children safely evacuated, the 39-year-old dentist worked up to twelve hours a day in several practices. During any spare time he could create, he did his bit for the war effort. His job was to help 'clear up' after the bombing raids. He hated the work which he described as 'picking up bits and pieces of dead bodies'. John was so nauseated by the carnage that eventually he could no longer continue to sift through the wreckage. Not wanting to appear a coward before his fellow volunteers, John gassed himself.

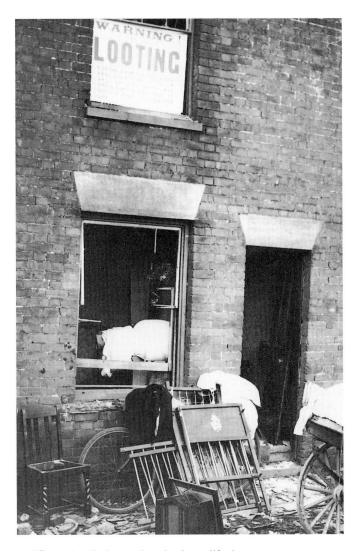

19. (a) and (b) Although looting was punishable by death, the sentence was never carried out. It was often difficult to know who were the real owners .

Bits and pieces of a dead body were discovered in a Baptist church in South London.

MURDER IN THE BAPTIST CHURCH

"I stood the stone on its edge. Underneath I saw some human remains. The head was nearest the steps. I noticed some of the bones were missing. I noticed some white substance round the bones."

As a demolition worker in the Summer of 1942, Benjamin Marshall must have unearthed a number of bodies mutilated during the bombing. This one was different. The ears, nose and fingers were missing and the teeth on the lower jaw were damaged. Benjamin informed the police of his gruesome discovery in the bomb-damaged Baptist church in Vauxhall Road, South London.

The blackout and bombed houses considerably assisted all those engaged in a life of crime or with old scores to settle. With thousands dying as a result of bombing, what better time was there to dispose of a body? These thoughts must have occurred to the ARP worker Harry Dobkin, who had been pestered for maintenance by his wife Rachel for nearly twenty years.

Their marriage in 1920 had not lasted long: three days, according to Harry, though his sister-in-law estimated some six weeks. Arranged in the Jewish fashion by a marriage broker, Harry said the union was doomed from the start. Despite this, Rachel gave birth to a son some nine months later.

With the couple separated so soon after marriage, Rachel's application for a maintenance order met strong resistance from Harry, who was a late and irregular payer, requiring constant reminding as to his responsibilities. At first payments amounted to £1 per week, but when Rachel went to live with her mother they were reduced to ten shillings. Despite this concession, Harold spent some time in prison for non-payment and was summoned four times for assault. He was an embittered man who felt he had more than paid for his mistake and after 20 years of doing just that, he planned the final payment.

On Good Friday, 11th April 1941, Harry arranged his own version of the last supper, treating Rachel to a meal in a small restaurant. On their way home he strangled her and concealed her body. He then made a series of fatal mistakes. Wanting to disguise the corpse as a casualty of war, Harold severed the head at the neck, the arms at the elbows and the legs at the knees. He then compounded his errors by depositing slaked lime onto the corpse in the false assumption that this would speed up the process of decomposition. Slaked lime, however, does not burn human flesh, instead it kills the maggots and beetles which would otherwise feed off it. Having thus inadvertently preserved the corpus delicti, Harry proceeded to inter it in the bombed-out crypt of a Baptist church.

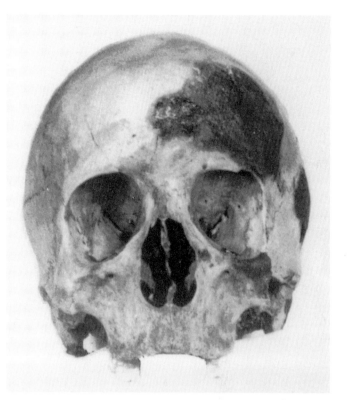

20. Full face photograph of the skull of the remains.

21. Photograph of Rachel Dobkin.

Rachel's disappearance was reported to the police by her sister on April 12th. Harry was the prime suspect. He, however, stated that following their meal he had seen Rachel take the No 22 bus to Dalston. Investigations were made and Rachel's handbag inexplicably turned up in a Guildford post office that same day. On the face of it, Rachel

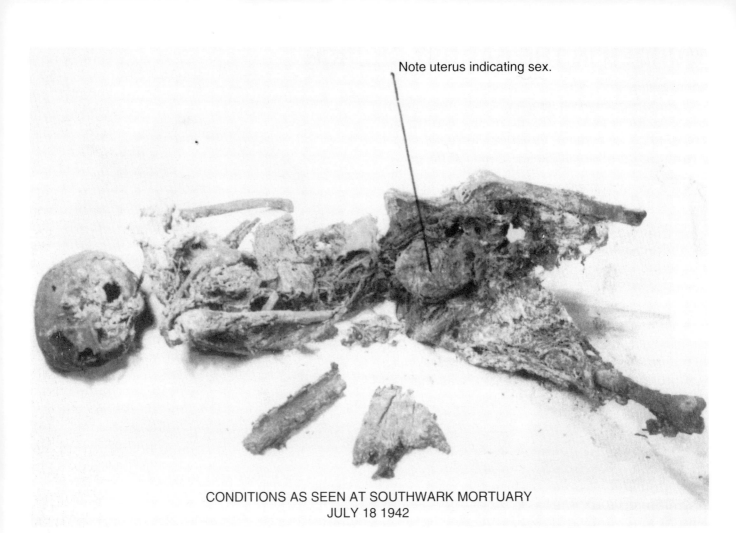

Note uterus indicating sex.

CONDITIONS AS SEEN AT SOUTHWARK MORTUARY
JULY 18 1942

22. Human remains from cellar at rear of Baptist Church, Upper Kensington Lane.

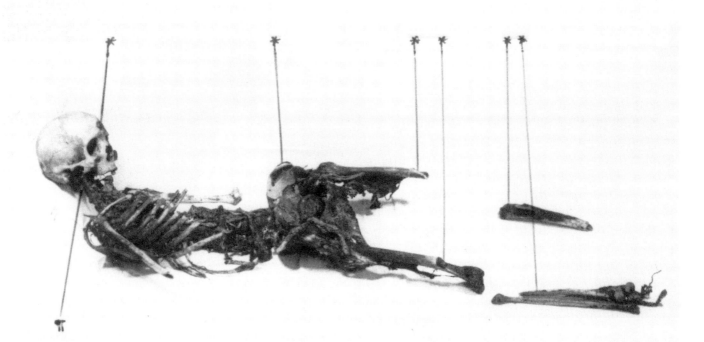

✷ Note Burned parts.
¶I Note also curve of neck and upper spine.

23. Reconstruction completed after study of soft tissue and debris.

seemed simply to have disappeared. In the upheaval and chaos of the times the matter was soon relegated to the back boiler.

Some fifteen months later Rachel's body was found. The discovery of the curiously well-preserved body set forensic experts on the trail. In a short while they had determined, from dental records, that the woman before them was Rachel Dobkin. When a married woman is murdered the husband is always suspected. Harry was interviewed in his new home in Dalston. When taken to the cellar of the church he denied ever having been there before, despite the testimony of the police witness, a boy, who said he had seen Dobkin in the crypt on several occasions. The witness recalled having spoken to Dobkin, who said he was there looking for coins. A police search of Harry's home unearthed lime of the same variety as that found at the scene of the murder. Harry was arrested and charged with murder, his only defence being that the body found was not that of his wife. Harry's mother wrote a moving letter to the Judge on 9th November 1942:

"Your Honor,

My son Harry Dobkin will be brought before you. I am unable to attend the hearing so I am asking you to be a father to my son. My husband and I are 83 years old and I a cripple. We both worked hard to bring our children up in an honest way without taking from charity or anyone. I wish to tell you my three sons were in the last war and one was killed.

Harry was at sea and was hurried into an unfortunate marriage by her people and when he found life impossible with her through the mental derangement he decided to leave her and support her although the family has always been a wicked jealous people and threatened to make him suffer all his life, he has only known prison through his wife. I know he is innocent of this terrible charge. If he had wanted to rid himself of her surely he had reasons from the commencement of his married life. Harry has the highest character from everyone who knows him and that's hundreds of people who have known him for years. He has always been the first to help people and also his wife who have always pestered him and our family. So dear Sir please impress the jury that Harry is innocent and give me back my son. We are so lonely and please don't send an old woman to the grave with this terrible disgrace on her mind.

Thanking you again my eyes are almost blind through crying.
Yours Respectfully,

Mrs. Dobkin."

24. Harry Dobkin took advantage of the wartime conditions to murder and dispose of his wife.

Mr. Justice Wrottesley did not form the same impression of Harry's innocence and neither did the members of the jury, who took just twenty minutes to find him guilty. When asked if he had anything to say before sentencing, Dobkin replied:

"Yes, the charge against me is very poorly invented. During the twelve hours of questioning at the Borough Police Station I was subjected to violence but I did not like to give evidence against the police. I hope I have not said too much."

This strange remark was Dobkin's last comment on the matter. It cast no doubts in the Judge's mind. Passing sentence of death, he commented:

"After a most patient hearing the jury has come to what I think is the right conclusion on this matter."

Harold showed no emotion and was hanged at Wandsworth.

PRISON FOR THEFT OF TINNED APRICOTS

25. *Pilfering from the docks was rife.*

Very few people could honestly say they spent the whole of the forties without 'bending' the rationing laws a little, even if only by consuming the odd extra rasher of bacon. Some professional rogues, however, saw the war not so much as a chance to help their country, but more of a chance to help themselves.

The Minister of Food announced, in 1940, that there would be no more bananas till after the war. Bacon and butter were rationed just months after the outbreak of hostilities. With increased restrictions on the sale of tea, margarine and cooking fats in 1940 and the introduction of clothing coupons soon after, more and more people were tempted into doing deals under the counter. Long queues outside shops became the norm. As they did not often queue for rationed food, however, people soon twigged that a large line up outside a shop meant the prospect of a treat in store. Many joined queues without knowing what they were for and sometimes found their wait rewarded with a tin of dog or cat food.

There were three main sources of supply to the black market, which grew rapidly during 1941-42:

theft and pilfering, illicit sales of agricultural produce by farmers and small holders and illicit manufacturing. The greatest demand was for black market meat.

Large quantities of food were pilfered from the docks. Vans would be deliberately overloaded, with the imported meat being sold on. If caught by inspectors from the Ministry of Food, offenders faced an average gaol sentence of between three and six months.

Many shopkeepers, with more than twenty years unblemished trading to their credit, were tempted by the high profits to be made. When people were away on holiday or had recently died, the shopkeeper might claim rations for them and sell them on to regular customers. One Enfield butcher received six months for passing off horseflesh as stewing steak. Inspectors in Hackney found workers loading tuberculous meat into a sausage machine. Another raid uncovered mounds of dropsical beef stuffed into sacks. Birds, ostensibly sold for breeding, would often end up on dinner plates.

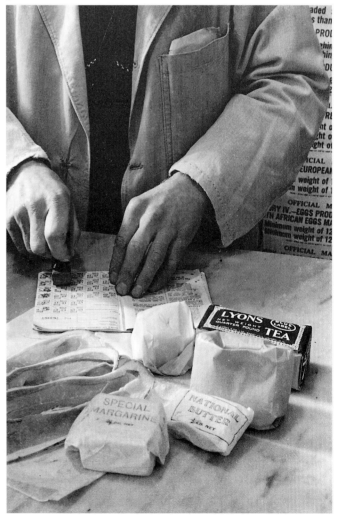

25. (a) *The coupons are stamped and one week's rations passed over. Nearly everyone dabbled in the black market at one time or another.*

26. London's Loot Alley. Returning servicemen sold the spoils of war in Cutler Street.

27. Queuing for fish, April, 1943. People often joined queues without knowing what was on offer.

Following the theft of a number of sides of bacon imported from Canada, three men stood in the court facing a maximum of five charges relating to the stolen meat. One of the accused had trouble following the proceedings:

CLERK OF THE COURT: "Knapfield, are you guilty or not guilty?"
THE PRISONER KNAPFIELD: "Guilty on charges 4 and 5."
CLERK OF THE COURT: "Goldberg, are you guilty or not guilty?
THE PRISONER GOLDBERG: "Guilty on count 4."
CLERK OF THE COURT: "Pribik, are you guilty or not guilty?"
THE PRISONER PRIBIK: "Guilty on count 4."
CLERK OF THE COURT: "You cannot be. You are not charged in that. You are only charged with counts 1 and 5."
THE PRISONER PRIBIK: "Count 5."

The prisoners received sentences ranging from three to eight months imprisonment.

Typical headlines from the local press read:

'Man jailed for corned beef theft.'
'Prison for theft of tinned apricots.'
'Bought beef but it was horseflesh.'
'Man with 13lbs. of pork loses appeal.'
'Bought underwear without coupons.'

Unscrupulous landlords in several London pubs substituted 'hooch' for whisky. This was an illegally distilled mixture of meths and chemicals sold to customers when the landlord judged them to be too drunk to know the difference in taste. At least one fatality was caused when a befuddled boozer leapt through a window and fell twenty feet to his death.

For some, the consumption of any black market food was a treasonable offence. Sir Waldron Smithers, M.P., wrote to the Home Secretary on 12th August 1942:

"Black markets are still rampant. These activities could be stopped in six weeks if the Government would have the courage to use the powers they now have, or take more powers to inflict more severe penalties...
Everyone convicted of black market activities should be liable to:-
1) The death penalty.
2) Flogging.
3) A minimum of 14 years penal servitude.
4) Deprivation of all property.
5) Deprivation of the rights of a citizen.

Black-marketeers are cowards, and a few drastic examples of shooting or flogging would end this scandal, which is not diminished by the pious utterances of ministers.
The recent example in America of the electrocution of six spies might well be copied in this country, both in spy and black market activities."

28. At least the pigs didn't go hungry. Police in Hyde Park, 1941.

30. Word quickly spread when clothes shops had been damaged.

Clothes rationing reduced people's purchases by 50%. With an allowance of just 66 clothing coupons per fifteen months - one man's woollen overcoat taking sixteen points, a pair of knickers, two - there was an insatiable demand. With only a small number of coupons difficult choices had to be made, these were the days of fur coats and no knickers.

With a general rise in wages and richer Londoners unable to spend abroad, a shortage of money wasn't the problem, a shortage of coupons was. Rich employers might swop food coupons for clothing coupons with their maids and then purchase their own nutritional requirements on the black market. Indeed for some, fashionable clothing was far more important than food. We've all heard the stories of how far some girls would go for a pair of stockings. Everyone simply grew bored with 'make do and mend'.

In June 1943, the police were called to the offices of the Customs and Excise in Victoria. The padlock on a cupboard had been forced and 40,000 clothing coupons were missing. The robbery was

29. (pages 28 and 29) A 1940 photo guaranteed to revive memories of wartime shopping.

quickly solved when police raided an office in Warwick Street. They interrupted three people in the middle of counting out their booty, one of whom tried to stuff the evidence down the front of his trousers.

By 1944, the black market value of one clothing book was about £5 or two shillings a coupon. Even after the war, travelling salesmen would knock on doors selling clothes and came to an arrangement for payment without coupons on the never-never. Clothing rationing did not end until 1949.

Following his discharge from the army on medical grounds, Henry Cohen determined to employ his business acumen by dabbling in the black market. He started out by buying stolen clothing coupons, paying £10 per thousand and selling them on in smaller quantities. When the stolen coupons were traced back to Henry, the police determined to search his flat to see if they could unearth any more incriminating evidence. They soon found out that Henry was not just into clothing.

The following foods were found stashed away. If obtained legally they would have used up both Henry's and his wife's complete rations for nearly two years.

Henry admitted he obtained them without coupons. The cache contained:

43 tins of beans (various sizes)	92 pts.
31 tins of chocolate coated biscuits	115 pts.
41 tins of sardines	141 pts.
12 tins of anchovies	24 pts.
12 tins of salmon (various sizes)	274 pts.
7 tins of peas (various sizes)	22 pts.
3 x 12 oz tins of chopped ham	54 pts.
5 x 12 oz tins of chopped pork	90 pts.
14 tins of fruit (various sizes)	93 pts.
Total	905 pts.

When petrol was restricted to just three gallons a day, taxi-drivers had to give up their old habit of cruising. They would stay at one stand and wait for customers. After the Americans arrived taxis were very hard to find as Yanks were charged up to three times the normal rate.

The police doggedly followed all leads in their pursuit of stolen ration coupons, no matter what time of day or night. At 4.a.m. on New Year's Day 1944 in Falmouth Road, just off the New Kent Road, two detectives were acting as if they were drunk. Thumping on a chosen door they began singing the opening refrain from 'Auld Lang Syne.' They threatened to continue singing until the door was opened. When the occupants opened the door to see what the commotion was about, the policemen instantly 'sobered' up. Pushing by the men at the door they forced their way into the dining room and quickly found what they were looking for: coupons for 209,000 gallons of petrol and a rubber stamp.

Judging from police notes about the comments made by Neil and Thomas, two of the three men arrested, they were evidently Laurel and Hardy fans.

Neil: "I suppose this means we shall be inside until 1948."

Thomas: "What a mess we are in. A nice start to the New Year."

Both men were found not guilty when the third occupant owned up to stealing the coupons and was sent down for three years.

31. Clothes rationing in 1941. High prices were paid for stolen coupons.

There was always a ready market for pilfered goods. The Hackney Gazette would conscientiously list goods that had 'disappeared' from factories, thus inadvertently informing the local inhabitants what would shortly be available. These items ranged from grosses of sanitary towels and 'miscellaneous' rubber goods to 66,000 knives, forks and spoons.

In Romford, an employee was randomly searched at the gate when leaving his place of work and found to be carrying six dozen bars of high quality soap about his person. Not all workers were so unlucky. There were ways of circumventing the gate search. When a lady whistled outside a cigarette factory in Hoxton, a shopping bag stuffed with smokes was thrown from an upstairs window.

Some Londoners managed to procure two different sets of identity papers and were therefore able to draw double rations. Following a drinking binge in Camberwell Green, one such citizen, a 45-year-old woman, was found to be carrying two sets of papers when searched. She was sent down for three months.

Not surprisingly, rationing was resented more in the post-war years than during the period of conflict. In May 1945 the bacon ration was reduced by 25%; salt and vinegar were at a premium, even if fish could be found. For the first time bread was restricted, and in March 1946 in Stepney, bananas, now back on the market, were still so rare they were selling for between 8d. and 2s. each, on the black market. Other contraband foods included eggs, at 1s. 9d. each, apples at 1s. 6d. to 2s. per lb. and poultry, which fetched a staggering 6s.-7s. per lb!

Londoners were forced to experiment with new foods. Whale meat was imported in ninety ton carcasses on refrigerated ships from South Africa. It was cheap but not popular. Magnus Pike claimed it tasted like cod-liver oil and many people were put off by the awful smell it gave out when cooking. Snoek-fish, once again from South Africa, proved no more popular. Horse meat, described as such and not masquerading as beef, was also experimented with by the more adventurous.

At times it almost seems that an entirely new language was invented to protect consumer interests. When a new consignment of precious toilet rolls arrived, for example, one circumspect Croydon housewife informed her neighbour of the event by shouting, "Boots have stationery in" over the garden fence.

By the late forties it had become a popular pastime to outwit rationing restrictions. The number of spivs grew and were tolerated because they could provide what the Government could not . For many, dealing in the black market was the first time they had knowingly broken the law. Despite the stories we hear about the wartime diet being healthy, it was also dull, and few should criticise those who had the odd lapse and tucked into an illegal plate of bacon and eggs.

32. Spiv selling stockings in Oxford Street.

One man who had no need to curb his appetite was the black-marketeer, Reuben Martirosoff, a.k.a Russian Robert.

THE EXTRAORDINARY LIFE AND DEATH OF 'RUSSIAN ROBERT'

Buying and selling in the black market was second nature to those who had spent their whole lives wheeling and dealing. They knew the rules, the value of goods, the need to deal in cash and the necessity to carry some sort of deterrent. Refugees and deserters from European and Commonwealth countries, living off stolen goods, covertly agreed prices and delivery dates with home-grown spivs and shopkeepers tempted into the lucrative market, which lasted well past V.E. day.

One man, who made thousands of pounds out of the wartime shortages, was Reuben Martirosoff, better known as Marty, or Russian Robert. The 39-year-old multi-lingual stateless Russian served an ideal apprenticeship in the university of life.

Reuben lost both his parents and inheritance as a result of the Russian Revolution. From the age of 13, he was forced to look after himself as best he could on the streets. He left his home in Georgia and headed for Constantinople. There he toiled for 12 hours a day washing dishes, scrubbing floors and waiting on tables in a cafe. In his spare time he dabbled in precious stones and by his late teens had become a proficient buyer and seller of gems.

The deals, as one might suspect, were not all legal and above board and when Reuben was informed that the Turkish police were showing an interest in his business, he quietly slipped out of the country. After wandering awhile in mainland Europe, he finally settled in Vienna. Here the police were a little better organised and the Russian spent eighteen months in an Austrian gaol for stealing diamonds. Following his imprisonment for a similar offence in Paris, Reuben, now 22, and with ten years' experience on the wrong side of the law, arrived in London with £2,000 - quite a handy sum for a young man in 1928.

The young Russian dramatically increased his fortune by travelling the length and breadth of the country, setting up sales and then substituting false gems at the last moment. Anyone wishing to dispose of stolen jewellery would contact him, as he always paid in cash and always worked alone. When, in 1936, he was arrested carrying stolen gems at Euston Station, Reuben continued his grand tour of European gaols with a six month sentence in Pentonville.

This 'bird' must have been particularly harsh as Reuben, by then, had acquired a taste for the good things in life. His wardrobes were packed with over 40 Savile Row suits and twice that number of shirts. He only ordered the choicest food, and, in his local Soho restaurant, would work his way

33. Russian Robert made a fortune and lost his life trading on the black market.

through the entire menu, eating three times as much as any other diner. At the conclusion of each meal he would lay out his diamonds on the table and meticulously inspect each one with a knowing and loving eye.

He did not lack for female company, either. Habitually carrying three times the amount of cash the average worker could earn in a year, Reuben Martirosoff was living proof that crime did pay.

On the day war broke out, Reuben's assets doubled in value. With so much uncertainty, diamonds could always be traded - they were light, easily transportable and would retain their value come what may. In 1940 Robert married the daughter of the cafe owner in Constantinople who had first given him a job. Fifteen minutes after the ceremony he was again arrested and sent down for nine months having been convicted of breaking curfew and stealing.

When released, Reuben, or Russian Robert as he had become known to the criminal fraternity, found employment as a greengrocer's assistant. There was not enough money in fruit and veg. to support his expensive lifestyle and he soon handed in his notice. He was looking for something a little more exciting. His next venture was gambling. He did fairly well as a bookmaker but disastrously as a punter, losing all his profits and a little more besides.

Short spells dealing in foreign currency and forged tote tickets helped replenish the coffers, but he soon returned to what he knew best, buying and selling jewels, many of which he bought from his continental agents. Reuben's wife, Yetta, left him two years after their marriage, complaining of his womanising. They were divorced in 1944 and Robert subsequently wed a dark, plump Russian girl who mothered his one and only child. A few weeks following the birth, Russian Robert was found in his Opel. He had been shot in the back of the neck. His body lay spread-eagled over the back seat. Blood oozed out from the near-side door. The bullet had passed through his brain and embedded itself in the woodwork.

By the very nature of his business, Robert was forced to deal with foolhardy and desperate men. Many of these had flirted with death throughout the war years and in the aftermath did not hesitate to use firearms in pursuit of their aims.

Marion Grondkowski, a 32-year-old Pole, spent most of his adult life fighting Fascism, firstly with the International Brigade in the Spanish Civil War and later with the Foreign Legion in North Africa. He travelled to England in 1943 to join the Free Polish Army and for the next two years served in a special sabotage unit. One of his best friends, Henryk Malinowski, had himself only known conflict throughout his adult life. As a teenager he fought in the defence of Warsaw. He later escaped from a German concentration camp and joined the Foreign Legion. Both men would have qualified for medals if they had not inexplicably deserted for a life of cold-blooded crime in London's thriving black market. Passing himself off as a Polish sailor, Henryk made a living in illegal currency transactions.

Having heard the stories of Russian Robert's wealth, he arranged a meeting, ostensibly to sell a large consignment of black market whisky. On the night of October 31st 1945, the two deserters got into Robert's car in Notting Hill. One, and we shall never know who, sat in the front seat, the other in the back. The man in the back was responsible for the shooting.

When it came to relating their versions of what subsequently happened, the two men were poles apart. Marion gave the following account of events:

"After we got in the car, Robert suggested going to a nightclub, but after we had gone a little way I hear a shot and I get like bells in my ears. I could not hear anything."

As the car was still moving, Marion had to reach over and grab the steering wheel. As he got out, Henryk threatened to shoot him too. Marion simply replied: "If you like, kill me now."

24-year-old Henryk told another tale:

"I sat by Robert and Marion [was] in the back. We go drive along slowly and it is foggy and then I heard a shot and then I see Robert's head fall forward."

There had never been any whisky, the sole reason for the rendezvous was murder and robbery. The two deserters made off with £160 in cash, three watches, two wallets and a signet ring. They were arrested when trying to sell the watches.

When sentenced to death, Henryk, who probably pulled the trigger, broke into a broad grin. They were hanged at Wandsworth on 2nd April 1946. The police subsequently closed files on several hold-ups and the murder of a fifty-six-year-old taxi driver. Frank Everett, also known as the 'Duke', had been found stuffed into an aperture at a disused pump-house near Lambeth Bridge. He was rumoured to have dealt in the black market and was probably shot after doing business with the two Poles.

Marion and Henryk were just two of the thousands of deserters holed up in London who were responsible for much of the crime.

34. Marian Grondkowski - fought in the Spanish Civil War and with the Foreign Legion and Free Polish Army before deserting.

35. Henryk Malinowski broke into a broad grin when sentenced to hang.

36. Just who sat in the back of the Opel and pulled the trigger will forever remain a mystery.

ABSENT WITHOUT LEAVE

Many servicemen took a few days extra leave or disappeared for a short time, often to sort out family problems. Most returned to their barracks, but several thousand could not face that prospect. They simply went absent without leave (AWOL), sometimes for years. Without ration books, many either turned to crime, especially on the black-market, or alternatively found somebody who would hide them from the police.

The muscular and heavily-tattooed 37-year-old, James Lawrence, went AWOL shortly after his evacuation from Dunkirk. He took with him a Bedford Army lorry and his rifle and ammunition. After eighteen years of continuous service, James changed into civvies and set up home with Annie Imhof in a top back room in Tooley Street, near where the London Dungeon is today. After a lunchtime drinking session, Lawrence, a man known to possess an extremely jealous nature, was in his small room seething with pent up rage. He had seen the woman he was soon to marry speaking with other men!

Minutes after she returned home, Annie Imhof was shot dead, from behind, with the stolen army rifle. It was established, from powder burns on the dead man's clothes, that the pathologically jealous James Lawrence then turned the rifle on himself. The Army's sole interest lay in the whereabouts of the missing truck.

37. Christian Street in the 30's. A deserter sought to spend the war in an attic 50 yards down the road. These houses were destroyed in the bombing.

Those found harbouring deserters were liable to be imprisoned themselves, as Elsie Fitzpatrick found to her cost. The following report, taken from a 1942 edition of the London Shipping Chronicle, ran under the headline:

'TRAP DOOR IN CEILING'.

" 'You have been guilty of the most disgraceful betrayal of your country, and you will go to prison for six months,' said Mr. Roland Thomas, the magistrate at Thames Police court, to Elsie Fitzpatrick, a married woman separated from her husband, who was charged with assisting to conceal an absentee from the Army on her premises at Bedford House, Christian Street, Stepney.

The soldier, a gunner, had already been charged and remanded for an escort.

P.S. Doarks said on March 16 he went to Fitzpatrick's address with other officers and heard voices, including that of a man. He knocked at the door and after a lapse of two or three minutes it was opened by Mrs. Fitzpatrick. He told her he was looking for an absentee, mentioning his name and she replied, 'He is not here, I have told you that several times before.'

CEILING CUT OUT

Continuing, the sergeant said the premises were searched, and it was noticed that over a large cupboard from floor to wooden ceiling a portion of the ceiling had been cut out to form a trap door.

"Owing to my size" said the sergeant (he is a bulky man), "I was unable to get through the hole and another officer managed to get into the roof."

The absentee, he added, was found on the rafters behind a chimney stack. He became very violent and was taken to Leman Street Police Station in a police van. The woman was also taken to the station and when charged made no reply.

REPEATED VISITS

Sergeant Doarks further said that he had been visiting the house repeatedly since April, 1941, the last occasion being on Saturday, March 14, when voices, including that of a man, were heard there. On each occasion that he had called the door was locked and bolted, and Mrs. Fitzpatrick always took about five to ten minutes to open the door, by which time the absentee had had time to conceal himself above the ceiling. There were no other means of entry into the roof of the two-roomed flat occupied by the woman. The man, he added, had been an absentee since January 4, 1941."

Sentenced to six months' imprisonment, Mrs. Fitzpatrick cried bitterly as she was removed to the cells.

MURDER AMONG THE CABBAGES

38. The lovely Miriam Deeley, murdered in an allotment by Gunner Kemp, a deserter.

Miriam spent her all too brief forty-eight hour leave with her aircraftman fiance, Bill. She had accepted his proposal of marriage a few weeks earlier. He was temporarily lodged at her mother's home in Wanstead, but Miriam had to report back to her R.A.F base in Kidbrooke.

At about 8.30.p.m., on Sunday 13th February, 1944, the lovely young radar operator, accompanied by Bill, set out on the first leg of the tedious journey back to S.E. London. When an air raid warning was sounded their bus driver refused to go any further. The couple then made their way to Bow Road Station and kissed goodbye for the last time. Miriam was now running late for her connection at Charing Cross and missed the direct train to Kidbrooke. Having telephoned base to report the delay, she decided to take the 11.25. to Lewisham and walk the remaining few miles back to base.

Arriving at 11.40, Miriam struck up a conversation with Margaret McGregor who was travelling with her brother. They were taking the same road and were only too delighted to have company. They were joined by a young, blond, moustachioed man in uniform who casually fell in step with the late night walkers.

Ernest Kemp had spent most of his 22 years in South-East London and must have been overjoyed when sent to Woolwich. With friends and relations in the area he had the ideal opportunity to go AWOL, which he appears to have done. His part in the tragedy begins:

"On Tuesday afternoon, 8th February this year, I was detained at Woolwich Barracks awaiting courts martial for being a deserter. At about 2.15.p.m. that day I left the barracks under escort and went to Charlton Park Road Army Dental Centre to have dental treatment to my gums. I went to the lavatory whilst I was there, and, as there was no guard present, I climbed through a window and escaped."

Kemp spent the following nights sleeping at London Bridge Station and during the days travelled by train in South East London. He bought a set of sergeant's stripes, commando titles, combined operational divisional titles and Army Physical Training Corps titles and had them sewn to his uniform by a tailor on Waterloo Road. For good measure he added a pair of Glider Wings badges and a pair of brass crossed swords. Wearing this strange assortment of decorations, Gunner Kemp had just finished a cup of tea at the A1 cafe near Lewisham Station when he saw Miriam and the McGregors approaching.

He spoke about the recent air raid and how he hated Americans. When the two civilians left them as they neared Kidbrooke, Kemp asked if he could continue to escort Miriam. She agreed:

"Yes, I don't mind your company as long as you're not putting yourself out."

Miriam's semi-naked body was discovered the next morning dumped amongst the cabbages in a Well Hall allotment. It had been covered with her WAAF tunic and greatcoat. Beneath, all that remained of her uniform was a pullover, shirt, collar and tie. She had been strangled with her own scarf. From drag marks in the earth, police were able to pinpoint the exact location of her death, some 70 yards away. Miriam had valiantly fought for her life and lost. In this same spot was also found the first clue - the imprint of a shoe, size 11.

Furnished with a description provided by Margaret McGregor, the police interviewed hundreds of servicemen. Kemp was apprehended because of his propensity for wearing medals and insignia to which he was not entitled. He was spotted on the platform at St Pancras Station wearing the Military Medal Ribbon and North West Frontier, Afghanistan and Palestinian medals, all from campaigns conducted before he was born. He was in possession of the victim's wallet, fountain pen and keys. On 22nd February, 1944, Kemp finally confessed to what happened in the allotment nine days previously:

"Whilst we were walking along I put my hand on her breasts on the outside of her coat. She kept knocking my hand away and said ,'Don't do that'. I could see she was frightened...I put my right arm behind her and placed my right hand over her mouth and pulled her down to the ground. She tried to struggle but she had no chance...I twisted the scarf round her neck and pulled it too tight. She went out and I felt her heart and found she was gone. I took her overcoat off whilst she was there. I got the wind up, being near the footpath, and dragged her up near the cabbages and left her there. I don't know what made me do it but I undressed her. I took all her clothes off but did not interfere with her. After I had taken her clothes off I saw her naked body and thought someone might see it whilst going along the pathway, so I put her tunic over the top part of her body and placed her overcoat over the lower part."

Kemp stole Miriam's wallet, containing £11 and some coupons, and treated himself to a shirt, 2 handkerchiefs and a pair of gloves.

Although he pleaded 'not guilty' at the subsequent trial, no evidence was called in Kemp's defence. The jury took just 15 minutes to find him guilty, although they added a recommendation for mercy. This was not acted upon and Kemp was hanged on D-Day, June 6th. 1944.

HERE TODAY, GONE TOMORROW.

Not all desertions ended in such tragedy.

With 20,000 deserters of all nationalities at large some two years after the end of hostilities, the Government announced that anybody surrendering themselves voluntarily would be given a fair hearing. There was no chance of an amnesty.

In Brixton, Fred was tired of living a secret life; he also wanted to marry. After his proposal was accepted he surrendered to the nearest army office to await his punishment, and so become legit once again. His case, similar to thousands of others, scotches the popular belief that desertion is inevitably linked to cowardice.

In 1944 Fred returned on leave to his Clapham home. He found his house bombed and his father and fifteen year-old brother - the youngest of eleven children - living in the ruins of the basement. His mother having recently died in a car crash, Fred lost all interest in the war and determined to help his family.

With no photographs of him ever having been taken, Fred could easily go to ground. He burnt all his army documents and thus left himself in the vulnerable position of having neither I.D. nor ration book. Fortunately he was never asked to produce either.

After working as a greengrocer's assistant on Waterloo Bridge Road for several months, he started his own business, selling fruit from a barrow outside cinemas. When fruit became scarce he would buy soda wholesale for a penny-ha'penny per lb and sell it for tuppence at Brixton Market.

After court martial in Germany, Fred was sentenced to two years' hard labour, reduced on appeal to eighteen months. It is unlikely he served more than twelve as sentences were reviewed every three months and very few completed their full term.

In the year following Fred's coming forward, another 837 deserters turned themselves in and 440 were apprehended.

The public were not as outraged by desertion as magistrates appeared to be. Deserters were often looked up to by fellow soldiers for actually daring to do what they themselves had contemplated. As for civilians, when asked for her opinion of deserters, one middle-aged East End woman probably summed up the feeling of most Londoners:

"I'm afraid I've no opinion about deserters. I'm far too busy looking after my family. But if they get away with it good luck to them."

It was not only deserters who told lies and kept secrets about their past.

CHARMERS, CHANCERS AND CHEATS

39. Most leave was spent in London; a good place to lose yourself...and your identity.

The war provided ideal opportunities for both men and women to assume new identities. Many conveniently 'forgot' they were married and bigamously walked down the aisle with a new partner. There were more than three times as many cases of bigamy coming before the court at the end of the war than there had been at the start.

With many girls refusing intercourse until the knot had been tied, unscrupulous charmers, posted hundreds of miles from home, would engage in whirlwind romances, arrange a quick wedding and disappear into the sunset a few weeks later.

Alfred Gray told the court, in January 1944, that he had joined the army to get away from his wife. As we shall see the Southwark woman he married was not the best of housekeepers, but then again Alfred was probably not the most interesting of husbands, given his Grade 4 Army mental classification.

The couple were married in 1922 and lived together with their three children in a Southwark slum until Alfred, at the age of 40, signed up in 1940. Four years later he stood before the Recorder facing a charge of bigamy. He explained his actions:

"I have lived with my legal wife for eighteen years, but she was filthily dirty. I joined the Army in order to get away from her. I had to wash the children and I could not stand it any longer...She used to gamble with the money I gave her and when I came home on leave there was only a jam jar to drink out of."

Alfred met Hannah Fleming in August 1943. He proved that the Army had been correct in their mental grading, by marrying her in Lambeth, not far from his Southwark home. The second marriage lasted only the short time it took Hannah to find out about the first. He cherished the few weeks they were together.

"I never knew what happiness or home comfort was till I met Miss Fleming."

The Recorder had doubts about the soldier's tales of his wife's alleged slovenliness and bound him over to keep the peace.

A MAN OF ACTION

One man who saw a lot of action during the war years was John Taylor, although his case did not come before the courts until 1950. He appeared at the Old Bailey charged with double bigamy. In fact he had been 'married' at least four times without divorcing. Five of his 'wives' were in court to hear the case.

John's friends said that the 51-year-old was looking for the 'perfect wife'. During his search he fathered 11 children and charmed scores of women with his 'honeyed' words. His first marriage, in 1925, lasted just three months. His second, surviving an unrecorded number of years, resulted in eight children. His third marriage lasted only two months, the fourth a little longer and the fifth just one week. When the case came to court, John was courting a young German girl.

His ability to deceive women with half-truths would have done any politician proud.

He told stories of his travels to exotic countries - he served as a cabin boy.

He boasted of his address at a Park Lane hotel - he worked as a kitchen-hand.

He bragged about the days when he used to be in the newspaper business - he sold evening papers outside Cannon Street Station.

Throughout the case he did not once glance at any of the five women who gave evidence against him. The defence came up with some original arguments in mitigation. Whilst serving in the R.A.F. John had fallen off a ladder and lost his memory. They sought the sympathy of the male members of the court with the observation:

"It will also be remembered that, in the course of the marriages, he has had five mothers-in-law."

John Taylor was sentenced to four years' imprisonment, but was freed a few weeks later on appeal.

THE MONOCLED MURDERER

The war provided unlimited possibilities for conmen and impersonators. Harold Trevor sometimes gave himself the title of doctor, but more often assumed military rank. Speaking with a cultured voice and alternately donning spectacles and a monocle, the 61-year-old charmer exuded an air of confidence and reliability. He conducted himself like a man who had seen a lot of service, and he had: in H.M. prisons. Initially convicted for the theft of a purse in 1896, Harold was the King of recidivists, who just could not keep his hands off other people's valuables.

In October 1941, Theodora Greenhill, seeking to sell her flat, opened the door to her killer. Mr. Marjoribanks, alias Atkins, alias Trevor, arrived punctually to view the property. He had gone through the proper channels, gaining permission from the estate agents and with his correct bearing, grey hair and monocle, easily passed as an ex-officer. Theodora relaxed and invited him in.

Her body was found on 14th October 1941 at her home in Elsham Road, Kensington. There was a severe wound to the back of the head and a piece of cloth cord (resembling a pyjama string) tied tightly round her neck. The wound had been caused by a blow from a quart beer bottle, fragments of which were left at the scene. The pathologist told the police:

"The blow on the head would have produced instant unconsciousness and it was in this condition that the strangulation was effected."

The motive was obviously robbery. Trevor filled a stolen suitcase with an expensive fur coat, a cheque book and a quantity of jewellery. Police found bloodstains in the bath and assumed that the killer had cut himself. More significantly, they also found fingerprints on what remained of the bottle of beer. Police circulated a description taken from a statement provided by the estate agent and a sharp-eyed policeman in Rhyl made the arrest.

Quite why Trevor had taken to violence at such a late stage in his 'career' is unclear, even to the murderer himself:

"I had no thought in my mind of using any violence whatever, in fact I have never used violence to any person prior to 14th October 1941, throughout my life...From what I now remember I got a bottle from near at hand, probably in the hall and for some reason, for why I haven't the faintest idea, I struck Mrs. Greenhill on the head. From the time I struck Mrs. Greenhill my mind went completely blank until I recovered and found myself seated in the downstairs kitchen."

Trevor's defence of insanity and loss of memory was not accepted and on 11th March 1942 the convicted man was hanged at Wandsworth Prison. At 61, he was one of the oldest men this century to face the drop.

Many women were in danger in their own homes, not always from strangers.

40. Harold Trevor, impersonated an army officer. At 61, he was one of the oldest men to be hanged.

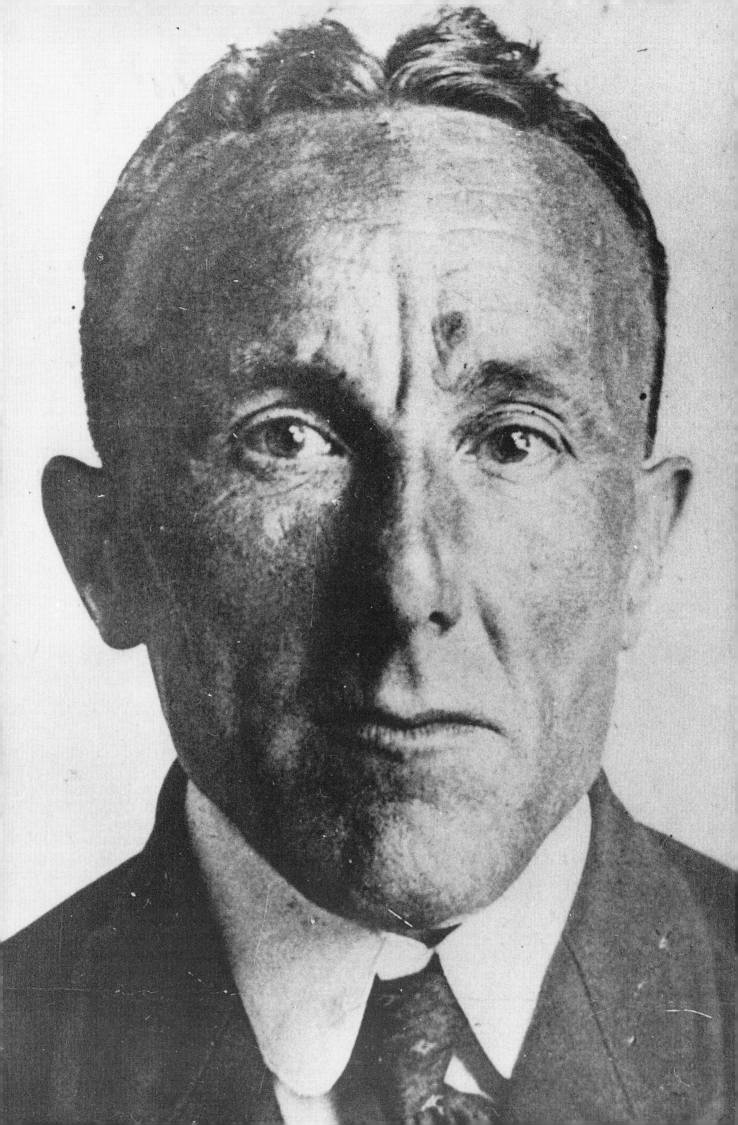

A RUDE AWAKENING

How often do surprise parties backfire and unannounced arrivals lead to more pain than pleasure? With the general uncertainty and disrupted communications caused by the war, many husbands and wives were literally in for a rude awakening.

After being invalided out of the Army in 1942, Quintin Hogg (Lord Hailsham) returned to his Victoria Street home unannounced to find his wife being a bit too free with an officer of the French Army. Hilda Vickers, for her part, returned to London from Scotland and found her neighbour sharing her husband's bed. He offered the tame excuse that his new partner had come to his room because she was frightened by the air raids. Hilda was granted a separation order and an allowance of 40 shillings per week.

Every soldier's worst nightmares were experienced by Sergeant Thackeray, who returned to his Camden Town home in the winter of 1944. He was not expected. Entering the living room, the sergeant was confronted by two women he had never seen before. They were sharing a double-bed with two black American G.I.s. Five of his six

41. Soldiers on leave at Victoria, 1940. Those who arrived home without telephoning were often in for a rude awakening.

children were imprisoned in the Morrison shelter in the same room. Thackeray went to his bedroom and finding it locked, began beating on the door. After much shouting and threatening, his wife, Lily, opened it. She was wearing pyjamas. Another black G.I. was coolly stretched out on the bed wondering what all the fuss was about.

Despite receiving an income from the army and an allowance from her husband's former employers, Lily Thackeray had converted the family home into a brothel, one highly-rated by her principal customers - black American soldiers and sailors. In her defence, 30-year-old Lily told magistrates that she had been led astray by the other girls, but they refused to listen. Five of the six children were placed in the care of the LCC. Lily was sentenced to two months' hard labour.

Pleading for custody of her offspring, Lily cried: *"Can't I claim any of the children - not my baby nor anything?"* The magistrate did not hesitate: *"No, I don't think you are a fit and proper person."*

Cuckolded servicemen often received a sympathetic hearing from the courts.

In Kensington a soldier beat another man so badly that he broke his dentures, lacerated his lips and caused multiple bruising. The magistrate let him off with a caution when it became clear that the injured man had been seeing the defendant's wife while he was away.

BETRAYED AND HUMILIATED

The 1942 case of William Needham, who stabbed his wife, is a classic example of the sympathetic treatment accorded to servicemen during this period.

When Police Sergeant Handley arrived at the scene of the stabbing in Poplar, he found Esther Needham lying in a pool of her own blood. She was bleeding profusely from a chest wound and receiving first aid from a police constable. Her estranged husband, William, was slumped on a chair close by. When asked what had happened he replied:

"I did it with a knife...she had it coming to her; she has been carrying on with another man while I have been in the army."

He produced a clasp knife from his pocket and added:

"This is what I did it with. I did it with a knife. She has broken up my home."

Esther Needham was too ill to attend the trial, the knife having penetrated her lung. The defence counsel argued that she had made no secret of the fact she was seeing another man - whom she called Alby - and had even introduced him to her husband as a prospective lodger.

It was probably as well that Mrs. Needham was still in hospital when the matter came to court, for comments addressed to the defendant by Mr. Justice Birkett would certainly not have aided her recovery:

"While you were serving your country you were betrayed and humiliated in circumstances which can be described as quite revolting...it was only at the last, when you were humiliated beyond endurance, your home broken up and the welfare of your children disregarded, you did that for which you stand in the dock to-day."

Needham's plea of not guilty to attempted murder but guilty of wounding with the intent to commit bodily harm, was accepted. Needham was sentenced to two days' imprisonment. As he had already served more than two days on remand he was allowed to walk free from the Old Bailey .

42. *Sergeant Thackeray arrived home in 1944 to find two prostitutes and two G.I.s in a bed in his living room. Five of his six children were in a shelter in the same room.*

"DON'T SHOOT HIM, SHOOT ME"

"This is a story of what is sometimes called the eternal triangle, where a husband finds his wife and lover together and shoots. It might be that when all the evidence is adduced the Judge may direct you to return a verdict of manslaughter."

With these words Mr. Christian Humphreys opened the case for the prosecution on 20th January 1942. Hanging on every word was Lance-Corporal Savos Constantine Savva who, charged with murder, faced the death penalty.

Savva moved to England from Cyprus as a 15-year-old in 1929. He married Iris six years later. The union produced two children.

The vast upheaval of war split the pair up. Savos joined the army and Iris and the children were evacuated to Norfolk. The country air seemed to agree with Iris, who flowered and chose a new man to complement the new environment. A short affair with a serving soldier, Corporal Cowan, was followed by a longer one with Fred MacCready, who was still awaiting his call-up papers.

Like countless numbers of evacuees before her, Iris, longing for familiar surroundings, soon returned to her home in Parfrey Street, Fulham. She had no intention of returning to her husband, however, and MacCready soon followed her. Meanwhile, Savos had heard rumours of his wife's affairs but during a period of home leave he told Iris he would forgive her. She would have none of that. She wanted a divorce.

43. *Many soldiers hoped their wives would be keeping the home fires burning. Some found other ways to keep themselves warm.*

During the following weeks Savos bombarded his wife with letters written in the torrid Mediterranean style. They were addressed to *'The light of my eyes'* and *'The light of my whole soul and body'*. She responded in the cold northern style: *'I do not want to see you again, so to avoid further trouble stay away. Under no circumstances will I ever live with you again.'* She could not have been clearer and eventually must simply have stopped replying altogether, as the following entry in Savos' diary indicates: *"When I see every other man getting letters and parcels from home, and I do not, I get depressed."*

Despite all this, Savos was determined to fight for his marriage. He applied for seven days compassionate leave and set off on a last ditch attempt to put things right. He travelled to London with his service rifle and, against regulations, five ball cartridges. Savos was to tell the court that he carried this ammunition in case of an invasion!

The enraged husband had not let his wife know he was coming home and let himself into their home early in the evening of 22nd October 1941. The flat was empty and after a short wait Savos went off to the cinema. He left his rifle and equipment in the sitting room. When he arrived back, his wife had still not returned so the soldier sat waiting in the dark. As he waited he loaded his rifle. When asked in court why he had done this, he said he had seen another man's shirt and cuff links in the sitting room and did not know if he was armed.

Savos was brooding in the dark when he heard the front door being opened at about 10.30 p.m. He heard his wife's familiar voice and that of a drunken man. They had only one thing on their minds and made straight for the bedroom. The man, MacCready, had been called up and was due to report for training the next day. This was to be their last night together. And it was.

Neither of the inebriated lovers guessed that an agitated and temperamental man was eavesdropping on their foreplay in the next room. Taking off his boots, he crept to the bedroom and, through a crack in the door, saw his wife on the bed with 'a man lying over her'. To witness his wife making love with another man in his own bed was too much for Savos. He burst into the room, pointed the rifle at the couple and screamed:

"What are you doing here? Get out of the house."

Iris struggled to get hold of the barrel of the rifle. She pleaded:

"Don't shoot him, shoot me."

Fred MacCready then got a hand on the weapon and shouted above the din:

"Shoot me, not her."

The struggle lasted for almost ten minutes, during which time MacCready is said to have inadvertently released the safety catch. Both men were bruised and bleeding and one of MacCready's eyes was badly swollen. Iris rushed into the kitchen as Savos finally managed to wrestle control of his weapon. The lance corporal then went in pursuit of his wife. After overcoming her lover, Savos stood face to face with the woman he had once worshipped, but now detested. She stood naked, vulnerable and very frightened before a man supercharged with hate.

A neighbour later testified:

"There was a noise as of a bursting tyre and then silence."

Whether Savos shot Iris accidentally or deliberately only he knows. The bullet passed through her arm, through her body, through the kitchen and lavatory and into the garden where it was found. Death was instantaneous.

The prosecution argued that Iris, knowing in her last few seconds of life that she was going to be shot, had folded her arms across her chest to protect herself. This was the reason the bullet had passed through her arm.

Savos sunk to his knees and cradled the dead woman's head in his lap. He shouted for someone to get a doctor. MacCready meanwhile did not hang about, but fled with the parting words: *"Look what you've done now, you fool!"*

The first policeman on the scene testified that he found the dead body of Mrs. Savva on the landing, lying in a pool of blood. Savos was standing nearby. When asked what had happened he made no reply. A rifle with the magazine missing lay discarded on the bedroom floor. Savva produced the magazine with four cartridges from his pocket. After being cautioned he simply said:

"I did not shoot my wife. It happened accidentally. I was struggling with the other fellow."

Savva stuck to his story at the police station:

"I did not intend to kill my wife. I love her and only intended to frighten her."

Given the opening words of the Crown, it appeared that prosecuting counsel were not pressing for a conviction for murder. This is further illustrated by Mr. Humphreys summing up:

"If a man finds his wife with a lover and in his fury and red anger kills one of them on the spot, the charge may be reduced to manslaughter."

After fifty minutes deliberation the jury agreed on the manslaughter option. Savos Constantine Savva was gaoled for fifteen months.

44. On occasions the rifle was turned on a wife or her lover.

SHOOTING TO ENDANGER PUBLIC LIFE

Arthur Warren, a lance corporal in the Black Watch, had been married for eight years, the last three spent in the army. His statement to the police was read out at the Old Bailey in November 1944:

"We have a child, a boy aged four. We were quite happy and lived a normal married life. I was called up in January 1942 and am still serving. I was in France and while there began to suspect my wife because I had only two letters from her during the period I was there. I returned from France in August, 1944 , and went to a public house and there I saw her with the man I now know as Pomroy. I spoke to my wife and said:
'We are going home now.'

I didn't even know the address. My wife left with me leaving Pomroy in the public house. She didn't want to go at first but eventually she took me to where she was living in Cantrell Road, Bow. She told me she had finished with me. She said she was friendly with other men and wanted a divorce. I tried to talk her around and said I would forgive her anything for the boy's sake, but she persisted in her desire for a divorce.

She would have nothing more to do with me, so I left her and went to my mother's flat. Since then I have seen my wife four or five times with a view to reconciliation but she would not listen.

On November 5th I came home on embarkation leave for seven days. With authority I had my army rifle and some odd rounds of ammunition. About midnight I went to Cantrell Road with the object of scaring my wife and also seeking grounds for divorce. I still had my rifle and ammunition with me.

Evil thoughts entered my mind but I dismissed them.

When I arrived at the house I knocked at the door. My wife came to the door but did not open up. I told her who I was and all she did was to shoot the bolts. The letter box was open and through it I saw the kitchen light was on and I could see Pomroy in the kitchen. Pomroy was partly dressed and I saw my wife go and join him. I then broke in a panel of the door with my rifle butt and entered the house.

Pomroy and my wife ran into the yard and I followed them. As I reached the yard Pomroy jumped at me and struck me in the eye. I dropped my rifle and tried to protect myself and we exchanged blows. My wife took up the rifle and threatened to hit me over the head. I broke away from Pomroy and snatched the rifle from her. I stepped back a few paces and opened the bolt of the rifle and put a round in the breach and fired in the air....If I wanted to shoot anyone I could have shot them when they were in the kitchen."

Charged with shooting to endanger public life, the lance corporal, who had been given impeccable character references by the Army, very much hoped his version of events would be believed.

The sequence of events put forward by the prosecution was at odds with Arthur's statement. Neighbours testified that they intervened to break up the fight and when Arthur appeared to have calmed down he was handed back his rifle. A short time later they heard a shot. It was not into the air, however, as it struck a doorway at the height of 3' 2" near where Pomroy was standing. Arthur was heard to say:

"While I have been fighting for my country this is what I come back to find."

These words may well have struck a chord with the members of the jury as Arthur was found not guilty and discharged.

45. The sort of cosy domestic scene most soldiers dreamed about. In reality many of the dreams turned to nightmares.

46. *Black G.I.s were pleasantly surprised at the welcome they received from English girls.*

ONE WEDDING, ONE FUNERAL AND FIVE YEARS IN PRISON

Three days after his wedding, 41-year-old James Turner gave police a chilling account of the morning he murdered his bride of 72 hours. Lilian Hinton, a telephonist employed by Peake Freans, told James she wanted to have his baby. Despite the misgivings of Lilian's mother they were married on special licence at Bermondsey Town Hall on Friday 27th July 1942:

"I have known my wife since July 1941. Her name was Lilian Emily Hinton.

I told her I was 33. We became very friendly and we used to go out together. Eventually I was called up on 10th September 1941 and just prior to that we became engaged. I saw her from time to time when on leave. On several occasions when home on leave I was told by means of anonymous letters I received that Lilian was sleeping with other men. I put this to Lilian but she denied it....

We went to bed in the usual way and got up soon after 7.a.m. today. I told her that I expected her to play the game by me whilst I was away otherwise I would shoot her. She said that I would never regret

marrying her, that she had always been faithful to me and that she would like to know who was putting the rumours round about her.

I then picked up my rifle and put five cartridges in it. I wasn't supposed to have them but I brought them home as a souvenir. I then pointed the rifle at her side and before I knew what I was doing I fired a shot at her. I was about two yards away from her. I was standing by a chest of drawers and she was sitting on a chair facing the table with her back to the door. I shot her and she screamed, got up, stumbled to the fire-place and fell to the floor.

I then tried to shoot myself. I put the butt of the rifle on the floor, pointed the muzzle at my left side, leaned over and pressed the trigger with my right hand."

Because the rifle shifted at the last second Turner received only superficial wounds. He was found by his brother-in-law. The Judge was convinced by the medical testimonies that the suicide attempt had been genuine and sent the distraught serviceman to prison for five years for manslaughter. His last words in court were:

"I loved my wife and my only wish was to be with her."

"I HAVE DONE A MAN IN WHO I FOUND WITH MY WIFE."

Thomas South, a Royal Engineer, heard of his wife's infidelity whilst he was serving in India in 1946. In response to a request for compassionate leave, he was sent to a unit in Britain. He argued, cajoled and pleaded with his estranged wife over three days but she was insistent. He was to see neither her nor their two children again. The brooding soldier went to live with his mother in Poplar. He could neither forgive nor forget and again tried to effect a reconciliation the following month.

Knowing his wife was seeing another man, South's hatred for the couple festered. Matters were brought to a head when he was shunned by his children who, following their mother's instructions, refused to talk to him in the park. Thomas, on the pretence of wanting to give his sons some pocket money, went to a flat in Modena Street, Paddington, where his estranged family was then living. Here his wife had set up home with her lover, 47-year-old Herbert Joyce. South, who was sixteen years his rival's junior, told the court what happened next:

"I went expecting to find my wife and two children in the house. I could get no reply to my knocking but my wife is a little deaf so I got in through a window, I opened the bedroom door and a man stood there with a torch in his hand. I guessed it was Joyce. I said to him 'You are just the man I want to speak to.' He hit me on the jaw. I rushed at him and held his arms tightly by his side. He then lifted his leg and kneed me. He put his fingers in my eyes and mouth and I started hitting him....Then the man clinched with me again, my wife was on my back. I could feel my little son's hands banging me on the head. I was forced onto the bed and I grabbed the man by the throat...I wasn't trying to kill him. I only wanted him unconscious."

Sarah Burns, a neighbour, disturbed by the screams, gave a slightly different version of events:

"In the bedroom I saw the accused on top of a man. I got hold of him and tried to pull him away. He told me to wait five minutes and the man would be dead. One of the little boys was holding a torch. South was grasping the man round the neck. During the whole of five minutes the man didn't move, he was lying still and I didn't see him struggle. South then left the house."

He later surrendered himself to two railway policeman at Westbourne Park Station in South-East London, near the excellent stadium, The Valley, home of **Charlton Athletic Football Club**. He told the men:

"I have done a man in who I found with my wife."

The defending counsel argued:

"This small sergeant was betrayed by his wife. Caught with Joyce he lost his wits completely and killed him."

The only problem facing the jury was whether they should convict for murder or manslaughter. In his summing-up the Judge referred to the particular difficulties of the times:

"Unhappily in the course of the anxious and troubled years through which we have lived - years of enforced separation between husbands and wives - there have been many cases where the temptation of separation has proved too much for one or the other. However bitterly a man may resent the infidelity of a wife, or a wife may bitterly resent the infidelity of a husband, that is no justification in law to allow an injured party to take the law into his own hands and take a human life. You will ask yourselves whether this is a deliberate, intentional and premeditated murder."

Thomas Smith had literally taken the law into his own hands and throttled Herbert Joyce. After a lengthy trial the jury found him not guilty of murder but guilty of manslaughter. He was sent down for five years.

47. G.I.s wasted little time in getting to know the locals. Problems arose when they didn't use their rubbers and girlfriends sought out backstreet abortionists.

48. (overleaf) U.S. troops parading through London, September 2nd 1942. With some two million young men passing through Britain confrontation was guaranteed.

THE AMERICAN
OCCUPATION
OF LONDON

The idea of American servicemen being overpaid, oversexed, overfed and over here was for the most part true. Receiving more than three times the pay of their British brothers-in-arms, and three times the civilian meat ration, and with access to many rare luxuries, including the highly valued stockings and chewing gum, G.I.s were sought after by friend and foe alike.

Being underpaid, underfed, undersexed and under Ike, British soldiers resented the brash self-confidence of rookie G.I.s who had never faced a bullet fired in anger. Both nationalities would wind the other up, but American jibes hurt most:

"Gimmee a beer as quick as you got out of Dunkirk."

At other times they offended the locals with such taunts as :

"I hear the British flag has four colours: red, white, blue and yellow."

Experts estimated that the average mental age of U.S. Army personnel in the first war was 12 years, in the second it was between 13 and 14.

FLEECING THE YANKS

G.I.s stationed in the remoter areas of East Anglia would often blow half of their salary on 24 hour passes to the capital. There was no shortage of prostitutes, conmen, black-marketeers, thieves and taxi-drivers waiting to welcome them with open arms as they stepped off the trains.

U.S. servicemen arriving at Ilford Station in 1944 would be met by bogus taxi-drivers, transported to secluded areas, relieved of their valuables and left to make their own ways home. This ruse was employed at least seven times before the offending gang was caught and sentenced to twenty-one months' gaol.

Most offences were alcohol-related. Curtis Moore from Virginia had a 'Mickey Finn' introduced to his drink and regained consciousness at the local police station minus £7. He was one of several such victims, but even the servicemen determined not to be hoodwinked made fools of themselves. A bottle of whisky on the black market cost somewhere in the region of £5, if bought legally (when obtainable) it fetched about £1. When offered the liquor at the lower price it was common for G.I.s to refuse it saying he only wanted "the real stuff".

In 1944, a 28-year-old barmaid called Julia Scott was sentenced to six months hard labour for obtaining £22.10s.0d. from six servicemen, four American and two British. Her ruse worked every time. On each occasion she picked up a man in a bar, hailed a taxi and promised her pick-up a night he would never forget. Arriving at a hotel, she told

her partner the number of the room and he handed over the money for services he was about to receive...or so he thought. Saying she was right behind him, she would usher the gullible punter into the hotel and make off in a taxi.

Detective Monahan said that he had received over fifty complaints about the woman who always directed her 'friends' to the same room. Referring to the success of Julia's ploy he observed:

"In many cases they were servicemen who were left practically destitute. She is illiterate and can hardly read or write, but she is extremely plausible."

49. *Jitter-bugging by the Serpentine on 4th July.*

Cecilia Beresford, alias Gladys Pembroke made her seventeenth appearance before the court in the same year. She too specialised in stealing from servicemen and was charged with stealing a watch and wallet from an American Air Force officer.

Defending a suspect with sixteen previous convictions would tax the most imaginative counsel. Guilt was not denied but in an effort to explain his client's actions the defence argued that whenever Cecilia went to the West End (she came from East London) a form of mania seized her and she could not help herself!

Unfortunately this is exactly what she did do.

Cecilia was sentenced to six months.

Corporal Clarence Rogers of the U.S. Army was strolling arm in arm with a young English girl down Staines Road in Harlow. On this warm summer's day the couple were in their own little world engaged in lover's small talk, the war of no significance.

Alan Piper, an 18-year-old labourer, was seething with rage. Both he and his friends had been humiliated the previous day in a fight between the local yobs and American soldiers. One of the yobs needed hospital treatment for a stab wound.

The inadequate teenager crossed the road and bluntly confronted Rogers:

"Are you a Texan?"

When he heard a negative reply he was not deterred from his intended course of action:

"That makes no difference."

He then punched the American on the jaw. In court Piper explained his aggression:

"I had a grievance against Yanks...I saw a Yank with a girl, I went up, took a fancy to have a go at him and let him have it...I told him if he and his boys didn't lay off the knives they would all get the same."

He was fined £2.

Fighting between the local population and their allies continued after the war. When an American soldier had his face slapped by a woman in a pub in Wembley, in September 1945, he immediately retaliated. Two British servicemen intervened and threw the G.I. into the streets. Like the cowboy he was he went for his gun, re-appeared a short time later and shot one of his attackers in the leg. He was given six months hard labour and reduced in rank.

DISHARMONY WITHIN THE RANKS

The G.I.s didn't just bring their chewing gum and candy bars to the streets of London, they also brought their racial prejudice.

Learie Constantine, later to become Sir Learie, was asked to leave the Imperial Hotel after American guests threatened to cancel their reservations. The manageress would probably not have made the diplomatic corps:

"We are not going to have all these niggers in our hotel. If he does not go tomorrow morning, his luggage will be put outside and the door will be locked."

50. The famous Rainbow Corner Club for American servicemen.

51. Black and white G.I.s were strictly segregated. The whites, especially from the South, resented the fact that English girls dated black soldiers.

The case when a group of white American officers refused to share a restaurant with an African trade delegate, who had been in London for several years, was discussed in cabinet. Churchill, who would certainly never have passed any test for political correctness, suggested giving the African a banjo, the Americans would think he was one of the band.

Black Americans were fighting two wars, one against Nazi Germany and the other against racism in their own army. British girls dated black soldiers and showed them hospitality and respect.

Many whites from the southern states, where segregation was endemic, called these women 'nigger lovers' and refused to have any dealings with them.

The SOS commander in London, General Pleas B Rogers, privately admitted that in London:

"The negro British nationals are rightly incensed. They undoubtedly have been cursed, made to get off the sidewalk, leave eating places and separated from their white wives by American soldiers."

52. *Inside the Rainbow Corner.*

OVERSEXED

Crimes by American servicemen were generally hushed up by mutual consent and often not reported in the local paper. With up to one and a half million red-blooded American servicemen in Britain just prior to D-Day it was statistically certain that serious breaches of the law would occur.

The Americans took responsibility for the crimes committed by their service personnel under the United States of America (Visiting Forces) Act of 1942. One of the clauses read:

'No criminal proceedings shall be prosecuted in the United Kingdom before any court of the United Kingdom against a member of the military or naval forces of the United States of America.'

The main difference between British and American law was that rape was a capital offence in the States and eight servicemen were hanged on British soil after committing this offence. Most also murdered their victims who ranged from a woman in her ninth month of pregnancy to a 75-year-old pensioner. All six hanged in mainland Britain were black. Whether a white serviceman would have been hanged for rape is open to conjecture

Servicemen charged with offences were sent to an American prison in Shepton Mallet, those charged with serious offences including murder, rape and sodomy being segregated from those facing lesser charges.

Not every serviceman convicted of rape was hanged. If the rapist knew his victim, had been engaged in heavy petting and then would not take 'no' for an answer he received a lesser sentence. If the man did not know his rape victim and used a considerable amount of force (and was black, some may argue) he was quickly and permanently disposed of. There were several differences between the British and American hanging rituals.

Americans were hanged at 1.a.m., following a hearty meal and farewell party. The condemned man had access to as much canned beer as he could drink and the very best of available food. The party continued, albeit without the host, after the hanging. In Britain the final meal was traditionally a sombre affair. Under British law, once a man reached the execution room he was dispensed with as speedily as possible. Americans, however, were forced to stand on the drop for up to six minutes, whilst the charges were read a final time.

53. Pink satin camiknickers embroidered with the American flag on sale at Lillywhites in September 1942.

54. *Snowdrops arresting an offender in Park Lane. There were serious disturbances when men on leave couldn't hold their liquor.*

Some of the murders committed by American servicemen occurred in the Greater London area. The following case fitted the familiar pattern of the jilted man shooting his former girlfriend, then himself.

38-year-old Private John Waters wooed Doris Staples, who worked in a dressmaker's shop in Henley-upon-Thames. From February until July 1943, the couple were very much in love and spent all their free time canoodling together. As frequently happens, however, one party, in this case Doris, decided to step out with other men. Word reached John that she was seeing other Americans.

On July 14th, John pumped five bullets into his former lover. He then fled to an outside toilet and turned the gun on himself. He fired upwards from under the chin, the bullet shattering his jaw, mouth and palate before lodging in his brain. Somehow he survived and made a slow recovery, losing the sight in one eye.

The local townspeople and several members of his unit submitted a plea for clemency but this was not heeded. He was hanged on February 10th 1944.

COWBOYS IN THE CITY

London was the natural destination for many soldiers going absent without leave. On New Year's Day 1943, Private Smith set off with a friend to see the sights and visit the cinemas in the capital. The two men stayed at the Royal Hotel, and Smith only returned to his base once his money had run out. Unfortunately, the whole unit had been transferred in the interim and the barracks left almost derelict. Searching the squad room he found a .45 pistol and armed himself. As he started walking towards the mess hall he was challenged by Henry Jenkins, a private in the 116th Infantry. Smith testified as to what happened next. From what he has to say it appears the mental age assessments may have been a little too generous:

"I did not know whether he was going to hit me or draw his pistol and shoot me. At this time the guard and I were about four feet from each other. As the guard made the motion toward his holster I immediately drew my pistol from under my unbuttoned overcoat with my right hand. All in the same moment I pumped a cartridge into the chamber with my left hand and fired point blank at

the guard's stomach from the hip position. When the first shot hit the guard he spun around to the right until his back was towards me. I then fired one or two more shots (I can't remember the number) into the guard's neck. After I had finished firing at the guard at my feet, I remained there for a few moments standing over him with the pistol still in my hand...I then holstered my pistol and ran away from the scene of the shooting."

Like in all good cowboy films, Smith would have liked to have ridden off into the sunset at this point, but instead he took the train to Paddington and was later arrested on Euston Station. He was hanged on 25th June 1943.

First prize for stupidity, however, must surely go to Private Alex Miranda, who not content with killing a man, had to draw attention to the fact. Having shot a sleeping sergeant, he boasted to his fellow G.I.s:

"Your worries are over now , boys. I have shot the 1st Sergeant and I'll turn on the lights so I can show you."

Court martialled Miranda was himself shot - 'sentenced to death my musketry'- at Shepton Mallet just one week before the D-Day landings.

55. American Army court martial. The Americans took full responsibility for the behaviour of their troops sent overseas.

SHOWDOWN AT CHARLIE BROWN'S

56. Charlie Brown's in Limehouse. The infamous pub was demolished in 1989.

There was always an atmosphere of excitement and expectation amongst the teenage girls whenever ships from the American Navy docked in the Thames. But pub landlords and local men had mixed feelings. They liked the money the sailors spent, but felt the pressure of always having to be on the lookout for hotheads who couldn't hold their liquor. When four destroyers docked in April 1944, and 4,000 sailors took to the streets in search of a little adventure, publicans went on red alert.

One of the most popular pubs for American sailors was the Railway Tavern in the centre of Limehouse, known by everyone as Charlie Brown's The bar was popular with British dockers and merchant seamen and was infamous with sailors of every nationality. A notice on the wall in the 1930's captured the atmosphere of the pub :

We have been in the business since
    1895
We have been pleasing and DISPLEASING
the people ever since
We have been cussed and discussed
boycotted, talked about, lied to
hung up, held up, robbed & c

The only reason we are staying in
business is to see
WHAT THE HELL
  IS GOING TO
    HAPPEN
      NEXT
       ?

When large groups of American sailors arrived, good-natured jibing occasionally got out of hand, which led to the odd skirmish or full-scale brawl; Yanks versus the rest.

In the back bar, on 11th April, a circle of American seamen had gathered and were 'yelling their heads off.' They paid little attention when the licensee pleaded, "come on boys, break it up." One of the locals showed his displeasure of the group of drunken loudmouths by lobbing beer glasses into their midst. A general free-for-all erupted and the licensee knew he had to take drastic action.

"Give me my stick" he shouted to his wife.

She quickly produced a 'heavy polished truncheon-shaped wooden implement.' Brandishing the club, he waded into the middle of the fracas cracking two of the combatants over the head. The police arrived and cleared the pub. An Irishman was taken to hospital by ambulance but otherwise there were no serious injuries, just wounded pride.

Later that evening there was a battering at the door and four American seamen rushed in but were 'sent flying' by the landlord and his newly-favoured weapon.

A 29-year-old lorry driver, Charles Gilbey, had chosen the wrong evening to make his first visit to Charlie Brown's. He generously helped the landlord to shut up at 10.p.m. Most people had forgotten about the brawl, but lurking outside the pub crouched a sailor seething with pent-up fury. He wanted to hurt someone, hurt someone badly, and he didn't care who. Showing tremendous strength, he lunged at the door and broke one of the panels. A long ebony-handled knife was recklessly and blindly thrust into the pub and sank deep in human flesh. Charles received the full force of the thrust, the knife penetrating some five inches into his chest, between the first and second rib. He died before any assistance arrived.

The only clue as to the perpetrator was that both the landlord and his wife saw the arm of the murderer and recognised from the sleeve that the uniform was that of the American Navy. A mob of sailors, loitering nearby, quickly dispersed and the authorities had the seemingly impossible task of finding their man amongst 4,000 shore-leavers. Amazingly, with the help of American officers, they found him within twenty-four hours.

That evening Harold Tipping, an American ship's officer, visited several Limehouse pubs to locate members of his crew. Returning to his ship he found second cook 'Slim' Geddes bleeding from cuts on the left wrist and scalp. He questioned other sailors and found that several of them had been at Charlie Brown's that evening. They openly

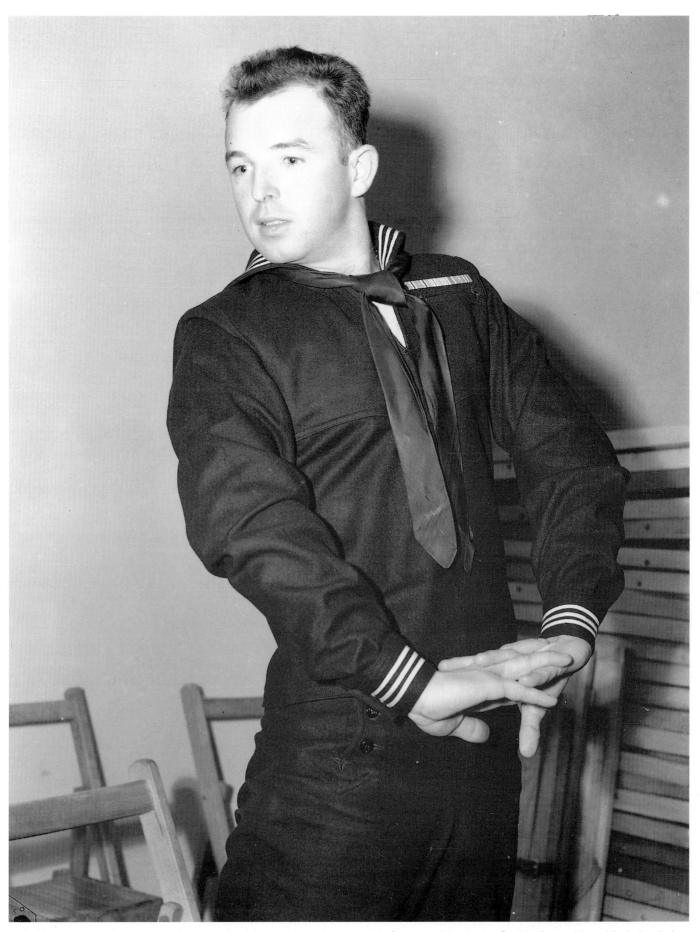

57. Condemned to death in the electric chair, 19-year-old Gunner Matthew Smith from New York had the sentence commuted to a long term of imprisonment in Sing Sing.

spoke about the fight and Lincoln Wiffrey told the officer that after the pub had been evacuated, he heard some of the seamen say that one of their men was still inside. He said he saw the frontal assault that was quickly repulsed, but he also admitted seeing a man run up from Garland Street and throw out his fist until it was level with the door. The man then left in a stooping position.

Officers from Scotland Yard circulated details of the offence to all the ships and the field was soon narrowed down. When a rating, seeking to clear himself, approached one of his superior officers and told them that the description of the knife matched his own, which he had lent out to Matthew Smith earlier, the authorities knew they had their man.

Gunner Smith was a 19-year-old from 38th Street, New York. At the court martial, held in a room on Regent Street, he pleaded not guilty to the charge of murdering Gilby and made the same plea to a further charge of carrying a knife concealed about his person without proper authority.

A Miss Avis Holdemann gave evidence saying that at 9.30 p.m. on the night of the murder, Smith told her that he did not have a knife on him but he did show her a knuckle-duster. Two sailors testified that Smith was not the man who made the thrust with the knife, though he was present. Lincoln Wiffrey stated the man he saw in the stooping position was dressed in civvies.

58. *Two of the attractions for sailors at Charlie Brown's: beer and a little female company.*

It was now time for Matthew to give his version of events:

"One fellow started kicking the door, and I stared kicking it too. The door broke and opened and we went in. A man came rushing at us with a club. He hit one fellow and I ran out. He closed the door and as he was swinging the club through the broken partition I made a slash with a knife."

This was the knife, it must be remembered, that Smith denied carrying. He added in his evidence that he did not feel the knife make contact.

Lincoln was a loyal friend and when recalled stuck to his story saying that the man he saw was thick set with black hair and was wearing a civilian suit - definitely not Smith!

Ironically the officer in charge of the case was also called Smith. Detective Inspector Smith told the court martial about his questioning of the defendant at Limehouse Police Station. Here the young sailor was reported to have said:

"If I tell you the truth you will hang the murder on me."

He was right about that. Found guilty, Matthew Smith was sentenced to die in the electric chair. Because of his youth, however, he did not face the death penalty but spent what should have been the best years of his life in Sing Sing.

Most of the murders were committed by American servicemen of the lowest ranks. They either had a sexual motive or were the result of petty disputes, usually fuelled by too much alcohol. The Judge Advocate General did not feel that the number of murders was excessive under the circumstances:

"Probably the majority of the murders committed in this Theatre were not significantly different from the murders which take place in the civilian community. It was virtually inevitable that an army as large as ours, representing a cross-section of the country as a whole, would contain some criminal, vicious and maladjusted individuals. It was just as inevitable that certain of these men, by reason of their own inherent propensities, by reason of human frailty in its various manifestations, and by reason of the whole complex of factors which normally produces crime, would commit murder or involuntary manslaughter. While ready access to firearms and the general tensions of wartime living may have increased to some degree the incidence of murders of this general type, it is felt that in the last analysis these murders were simply those which might have been committed by certain individuals in any large group."

The sole American tried for murder in a British court was Karl Gustav Hulten.

THE CLEFT CHIN MURDER

59. Betty Jones, striptease artiste and moll.

Sometimes war throws together individuals destined to bring out the darker side of each other.

Such a lethal cocktail was stirred with the meeting of a 22-year-old G.I. and an 18 year-old girl from Neath. Their mutual attraction resulted in disastrous consequences for all involved in their brief relationship.

Karl Gustav Hulten, married with a wife and child in Boston, had no criminal record, and had been a model son as his mother later confirmed:

"He was a good boy before this awful war began. In school he was a fine student with many friends. He never caused me a minute's worry until he became a soldier two years ago."

The army did not hold him in such high esteem, however, describing him as 'incorrigible and slovenly.' He had been 'over the hill' - absent without leave - for six weeks when he met the young Welsh girl.

Not even Elizabeth Jones's parents would ever have called her a good girl. Throughout her teenage years she had caused them innumerable problems, and would often hitch-hike long distances alone at a very early and vulnerable age. Elizabeth claimed that her invalid sister Gladys, a year older than herself, received all their parents' love and attention.

Elizabeth, who liked to be called Betty, was sent to an approved school until the age of 16 before entering into a loveless marriage with a childhood sweetheart, Stan Jones. The marriage was simply a ploy to prevent her from being sent back into care. As her husband went off to war, Betty left him to seek work in London. She would later accuse him of hitting her. After spells as a tea room waitress, cinema usherette and barmaid, Betty found work as a striptease artiste/hostess earning £4. per week. She became very popular with U.S. Officers and had a long list of their nicknames and addresses in her 'black book'.

Jones and Hulten met on 3rd October 1944. He told the immature blonde that he was a gunman from Chicago, the leader of a gang now operating in London. To support his story he showed her his gun and threatened to use it against her if she betrayed him. Over the next few days the disaffected deserter and thrill-seeking teenager set out on a reckless orgy of crime, culminating in the cold-blooded murder of a 35-year-old taxi-driver, George Heath.

George, like many taxi-drivers of the time, did a little dealing to help pay the £14 per week rental of the private-hire taxi. He dabbled in the black market for petrol and any spare profits he made were spent on gambling or his blonde mistress.

Like all other victims of random crime he was just in the wrong place at the wrong time. On 7th October, 'Ricky' Hulten and 'Betty' Jones were once again short of funds. With the deliberate intention of robbing the driver, they hailed a taxi in Kensington, asking to be taken to the end of King Street in Hammersmith. A fare of 10 shillings was agreed and the taxi-driver, the deserter and the strip-tease dancer set off on the short journey with vastly differing thoughts passing through their minds. George may have been thinking about the two young sons he doted on; Betty was possibly speculating as to how they would spend the proceeds of the imminent robbery; Ricky was fingering his .45 automatic, steadying himself to kill in cold blood.

61

As they neared the end of Chiswick Road, Hulten told the driver to stop. When George Heath leant over to open the back door for the girl to get out, Hulten shot him in the back. The bullet passed through the driver before striking the door and ricocheting into the dashboard.

Ricky pushed the driver, who was still breathing, onto the passenger seat and started driving towards Staines. Betty Jones rifled the dying man's pockets and removed some £4 in notes, about £1 in silver and some copper. She also helped herself to his wrist watch, fountain pen and self-propelling pencil.

Betty Jones, in a barely audible whisper, subsequently gave her account of events at the trial:

"The driver was still alive. Ricky told me to go through the pockets. I did not do it.

Ricky picked up the revolver from the seat and said, 'You heard what I said. I can easily do the same to you: if you don't go through the pockets I'll do the same to you.' He was breathing very heavily when I searched him. After a time he stopped breathing."

60. George Heath was murdered in cold blood.

George Heath, who had fought against the German Army and been bombed out by their Air Force, was thus murdered by an American serviceman, who was caught up in a vain attempt to impress an immature Welsh wanton.

The murderous pair dumped the corpse in a ditch near Knowle Green. Hulten claimed that they both lifted the body from the taxi; Jones said Ricky had dragged the still warm remains of George Heath into the ditch. With no drag marks being found at the scene of the crime, however, evidence seemed to support the American's version of events.

The callous couple drove the Ford V8 private hire car back to Hammersmith Broadway, and after carefully wiping off all fingerprints, went for a meal before going back to Betty's room. In her evidence Betty alleged that the following conversation took place:

BETTY: *"He is dead, isn't he?"*
RICKY: *"Yes."*
BETTY: *"That is cold-blooded murder, how could you do it?"*
RICKY: *"People in my profession have not the time to think what they are doing."*

The couple spent the stolen cash at the greyhound track and in the cinema.

Hulten was arrested because, either out of bravado or stupidity, he continued to drive the stolen car. He was spotted by P.C. Walters and when searched found to be carrying, in his left hip pocket, a fully-loaded .45 with a cartridge in the breach, ready to fire.

He told police at the station:

"I would not have been here but for that girl...if it had not been for her I would not have shot Heath."

Before the trial Betty wrote to Ricky in prison. The style of the letter suggests it was not for his eyes only. After warning him that her possible imprisonment would kill her mother she continued:

"What the police have against me is going through the man's pockets. Had you not ordered me to do so, I could never have done it. But as my own life was in danger, I did so. I could not believe you had done it, Ricky. You know the condition I was in for hours afterwards. I was dazed, and still you threatened me, even when you knew I was too scared to go to the police.

And there is another thing you must tell the police, as you promised the truth about the body. I did not help you to carry him to the ditch. You know that. Ricky for God's sake tell the truth. You and God are the only two who know of my innocence. Half of this case is fresh to me. The gun for instance - I did not know it was stolen...I did not know you were married and had a child. I did not know you had deserted the Army.

Why did you do it Ricky? And why have you got me into this? You are making me pay for a nightmare which I can't believe has really happened...If you have any respect, any honour, or pride, left, you will speak the truth, Ricky."

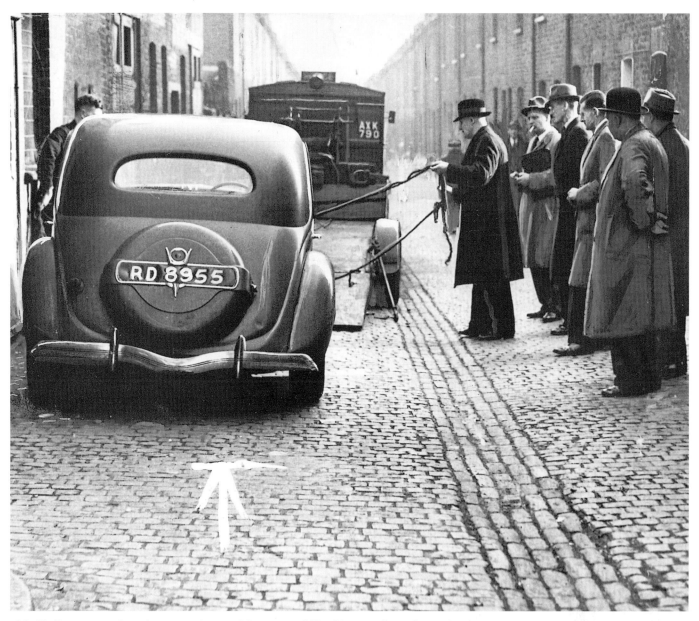

61. Police removing the car whose driver was killed by an American deserter.

Dubbed the 'Cleft Chin' case, after the Kennington victim's most distinguishable feature, the trial caused a sensation and throughout was conducted before a packed house. This was partly due to the unusual circumstances. Had Hulten committed the offence alone, he would have been tried by the American authorities: As it was he was the only American serviceman to come before a British court in this period.

Ricky's only defence was to claim that the gun went off accidentally. He began his evidence by stating that he was no Chicago gangster and then talked about the shooting:

"The pistol worked its way up from out of my belt. I had the gun in my right hand between my legs and my lap. As the driver stopped he reached over to open the door. As he reached over Mrs. Jones started to get up and I started to get up at the same time. My right sleeve caught on something on the door. What it was, I don't know. My arm jerked. The gun went off."

In the number one court at the Old Bailey, Ricky doodled as Betty gave evidence for over five hours. Her voice barely rose above a whisper. She told the jury that she was terrified of Ricky and that she saw him fire the fatal shot. According to Betty, everything was Ricky's fault. She in no way considered herself guilty and expected to be acquitted. Betty told her fellow inmates that Ricky would be convicted and nothing would happen to her.

She wrote this to her parents, whom she hadn't seen for two years:

"Now don't forget when you come to the trial, bring a suitcase for my stuff.
Also enough money for my fare home, just in case I haven't sufficient."

The jury of nine men and three women found both defendants guilty of murder. They recommended that Betty should be shown mercy but both were sentenced to hang.

After a futile attempt to grab hold of Ricky, Betty was led from the dock screaming hysterically:

"My God the _ _ _ _ _ _ brute, why doesn't he tell the truth?"

Details as to the couple's tempestuous days of violence leading up to the murder could now be revealed. Betty Jones was a self-centred, thrill-seeking moll, who willingly colluded in a campaign of violence against innocent victims.

Betty and Ricky had met on a Tuesday, spent the evening in the cinema and the next day drove to Reading in a stolen army truck. En route they picked up a girl and later dumped her by the side of the road after giving her a good beating and stealing all her possessions. A little later, Ricky tried holding up a taxi-driver at gunpoint, but was interrupted and had to flee empty-handed.

Later that week the pair stopped in their truck to 'help' Violet Hodge, who was struggling back to Bristol with some heavy cases. She had been to London to marry a G.I. only to discover that he was already wed. Violet only accepted the lift as there was a girl, Betty, already in the truck.

All three got out in a secluded lane after the American claimed there was something wrong with the back-axle. Violet takes up the story:

"Suddenly I got a crack on the head from what I imagine was a length of iron or steel. I fell, and as I lay on the ground, half-dazed, the man held me by the throat and tried to strangle me. I struggled and cried to the other girl for help. She just stood off laughing.

I lost consciousness then, and next found myself in water. It was the river. Swimming a few strokes I managed somehow to reach the bank and drag myself ashore."

Everything was stolen. When arrested Betty was wearing one of Violet's coats. She seemed to have a penchant for other women's coats. The day after the murder, Ricky brashly said to Betty *'Babe, pick out a fur coat, and I'll get it for you. Any one you fancy is yours.'* Betty pointed to a woman outside the Berkley Hotel in Piccadilly. *'That's the one I want.'*

Ricky approached the intended victim openly brandishing his .45 Colt. As he tried to drag the coat from the woman, she screamed and, as if to prove they do sometimes arrive when you need them, a uniformed policeman came to her aid. The disturbed assailants made their escape.

Betty would almost certainly have been spared the death penalty if she had been involved solely in the cleft chin murder. But the Appeal Court took the evidence of the condemned pair's mini crime-wave into account. This showed that Heath's murder was the culmination of a series of cowardly, cold-blooded offences of violence, rather than a one-off bungled robbery.

Whilst awaiting the result of his appeal, Hulten seemed entirely disinterested in his fate. He just lay on his bed staring at the ceiling. He showed no desire to do any exercise, nor did he play cards, read books or talk to the prison officers.

62. Karl Hulten shot a man to impress his teenage, Welsh girlfriend Betty Jones.

Meanwhile Jones, the striptease artiste, had found God. She wrote page after page of letters:

"God knows I have learned my lesson. I read my bible every night and I do love the Lord Jesus Christ...

64

God will answer my prayers, and I shall walk in the right path, the path which leads to God for the rest of my days."

When not pursuing her religious studies or fanatically dashing off letters, Betty would play draughts or the odd game of snakes and ladders. She smoked cigarette after cigarette as she repeatedly condemned the jury that, to her mind, had mistakenly found her guilty. She wrote:

"I would rather die than serve a prison sentence. God - what a jury! How I hate the London people. Hate them like poison. And how I hate that jury. Everything pointed to my innocence but they found me - guilty... Every time I think of it I marvel at myself for coming out of it without collapsing, although I nearly did in the end."

Both Ricky and Betty elected to attend their appeals, although they could take no active part in the proceedings.

Both appeals were turned down.

Betty only now began to realise the full extent of her predicament. Facing the prospects of being the eleventh woman to go to the gallows since the turn of the century, she devoted herself to religious studies and cut down dramatically on correspondence. When visited by her mother, Betty continuously sobbed, repeatedly asking:

"Mummy, mummy they won't let me hang will they? They won't let me hang will they?"

Betty's mother prayed. Her father organised petitions. Her only hope was a pardon from the Home Secretary, Herbert Morrison. It seemed the whole nation was similarly involved. Despite allied successes in Europe, which featured on the front pages of most newspapers, extensive coverage was given to the 'Cleft Chin murder'. Public interest was intent on the fate of the condemned eighteen-year-old and most correspondence regarding the matter was opposed to Betty being hanged, on the grounds of her youth. Clarence Burton, 34, offered to marry Betty if the Home Secretary decided to commute the sentence of death. He wrote to a newspaper saying he would wait for her and look after her.

Neither of the two condemned seemed to show a great deal of remorse for their victim. They appeared to have forgotten they had taken a life and were only interested in saving their own. When George Heath's widow was asked if she would join the appeal to save Jones she replied:

"Look at these tiny boys. They were devoted to their daddy and their father was devoted to them.

Betty Jones and Hulten killed their father...why should I forgive Betty Jones or Karl Hulten? They had no thought for my babies when they killed their father. I am afraid I have no compassion in my heart for them today.

I am indifferent about their fate. I have no particular desire to see either of them hang...but I will not lift a finger to help either of them."

Ricky spent this period staring sullenly at the ceiling. Not once did he ask about Betty. Betty, meanwhile, was having visions and bad dreams of the gallows and executions.

The Home Secretary communicated his decision just two days before the execution deadline. Dr. Malhieson, the prison governor, stepped into the condemned cell holding the piece of paper that would determine Betty's fate.

"This is it. This is your reprieve."

"Thank God, ' Betty started to cry and between sobs asked,

"What about Ricky?"

The governor shook his head.

Betty was removed from the death cell the next day and told she would probably serve twelve years. She became very depressed and spent some time in Holloway Prison hospital. Three different psychiatrists were assigned to her case. She slowly recovered and received scores of proposals of marriage through the post. One young clerk actually arrived at the prison with an engagement ring. Betty was released ten years later.

On the day of execution the condemned man usually changes out of his prison uniform which is then destroyed. He is normally hanged in the clothes worn at the trial, minus the collar and tie. As Hulten had worn his American Army uniform this custom was dispensed with and on 8th March 1945, Karl Gustav Hulten was hanged at Pentonville in prison attire.

In September 1945, the Ford V8 was exhibited in Somerset with visitors charged 6d. each to view the bullet marks. Several times a day, Violet Hodge told her story about how she was robbed and left to die. George Heath, of course, was not so lucky.

PICCADILLY COMMANDOS AND HYDE PARK RANGERS

63. The high demand for prostitutes led to the ten minute rule. Privates had to be paraded, stood to attention, discharged and fallen out within the allotted time.

"I particularly admire the little tarts who wander about the streets of Mayfair every afternoon and evening in their finery. When everyone else is hurrying for the air raid shelters they are quite indifferent and continue to stroll about undisturbed."

(General Lee, a U.S. Military attache, in a letter to his wife in 1940)

Although the number of prostitutes was estimated to have doubled between 1938 and 1945, the number of convictions for soliciting in 1940 was half (1,505) that of the 1938 figure. This was almost entirely due to the black-out during which couples were able to literally feel their way in the dark with less likelihood of being caught. Things were so out of hand that two officers from the Public Morality Council were solicited 35 times in just over 100 yards of Soho at the start of the war.

Some street-girls would sidle up to prospective customers in the pitch black and grab hold of their insignia to see how much they could afford. Others would shine torches on their own ankles and deliberately bump into soldiers and murmur, 'Hello Yank' or 'Hello Sailor' or 'Hello Dearie' and sometimes all three. It was business as usual during the Blitz; not only the Windmill could boast 'We never closed.'

Much of the activity was centred around the Hyde Park and Marble Arch areas and in Piccadilly. The girls were affectionately known as Piccadilly Commandos and Hyde Park Rangers, the main difference being that the Rangers gave an outdoor performance. Some girls preferred the park, as they were not expected to undress completely. George Orwell noted that the cheapest rates were to be found around Trafalgar Square, where prostitutes would do tricks for as little as 6d a time or a cup of tea.

Inspector Sharpe, of the Flying Squad, estimated that the girls worked an average four hours a day and entertained between fifteen and twenty customers, charging each between ten shillings and £1.2s. With shop-girls earning as little as £1 per week at the start of the war, the temptations were obvious.

Sometimes a change of air led to a remarkable change of character. Mrs. J was evacuated to the country with her two sons aged 6 and 4. There was much concern about the welfare of the boys following a report written by their Headmistress:

"She [Mrs. J] became a flagrant wanton and lived with one soldier after another. Boys in same bedroom. She took the 6-year-old boy out to cafes while she solicited. Looked like a first-rate tart. The child never had enough sleep, he was kept awake by his mother's affairs. In the end she started shop-lifting and her baby was born in prison."

The strangest part of this story was that a mother who knew her both before and after evacuation commented:

"She was such a nice respectable woman in Camberwell: never looked at a man."

BIGGER IN THE STATES

With a large transient population of refugees, deserters and foreign servicemen, the demand for prostitutes greatly exceeded the supply and the demand for services to the services rocketed with the arrival of the Americans. There was an initial problem with the supply of condoms, known as rubbers, to the two million or so Americans who passed through Britain during the war. In 1942 they could only obtain the British model, which they said was too small - well everything's bigger in the States! When their own supplies came through they would discard them in the churchyards, playgrounds and parks of the capital.

One G.I. remembers his Sergeant announcing at reveille:

"I'm told that we've got thirty thousand rubbers in the supply room. I want you people to do something about this."

Not all Americans were sex-crazed, brash and arrogant. Many came from small towns and were shocked by some of the sights in Piccadilly. One wrote to the Daily Mirror:

"We have been accosted by painted women more times in one night in Piccadilly than in our lives previously...by girls who should have been off the streets after dark because of their extreme youth."

By May 1945, G.I.s were being charged up to £5 for a 'short time'. There was such demand that many prostitutes imposed a ten minute rule. Privates had to be paraded, stood to attention, discharged and fallen out within the allotted time. Marthe Watts, a French prostitute doing her bit for the boys in London, had her own particular way of celebrating V.E. day - though in all probability it turned out to be V.D. day. Over a period of approximately twenty-four hours she entertained some 49 paying customers, only finishing work at 6 a.m. the following morning. We can only speculate as to why she didn't make her half century on this occasion, but overall she totted up over 400 appearances at Bow Street for soliciting.

PROSTITUTION - THE BEGINNING

For centuries young girls have been attracted to the capital and have resorted to prostitution to make ends meet. In time of war the demand for such services is almost insatiable. Behind most prostitutes there is a pimp, who often introduces the girl to street life and takes a hefty proportion of her earnings.

Jean Priscilla Hazel Jessop was tempted into hooking in July 1944, by 43-year-old Guy Armitage. Her story is similar to that of thousands of girls walking the streets.

Having been raised in an orphanage until the age of 16, the Hatfield girl worked for over two years as a housemaid and in an aircraft factory. Tiring of this employment, Jean moved the few miles south to London. She was an outgoing, brassy girl who enjoyed singing in pubs and simply just having fun.

64. *Very young girls were tempted into walking the streets. Here police check identity cards in the West End in 1946.*

Let's hear her story as related to the police, looking to convict her pimp for living off immoral earnings.

"I came to London 2 or 3 months ago to get work as a waitress. I got a job in a cafe and was there about a week. One Sunday morning I walked along Piccadilly to go to Lyons Corner House."

(Guy Hamer stopped and Jean accepted a lift)

"In the car he asked if I was working and if I had got any people. Then he said if you will live with me, I will get you clothes and furs and jewellery and take you to nightclubs.

I agreed.

About three days after that I started work for him at his suggestion. That was as a prostitute on the streets. The first few nights I earned about £7 nightly but after that I earned about £12 nightly. He paid me about ten shillings a day and paid for my hair to be done every Monday. While I was with him he treated me very roughly. He said I had got to make the money and while I was with him he hit me three times. He used to tell me I could go out on Sunday, my night off, and get drunk."

After three weeks, Jean moved out as Armitage

had found another young girl, with more earning potential, to move in. The pimp was eventually sentenced to a maximum of two years imprisonment with the judge adding that he regretted he could not order a flogging on account of the prisoner's ill-health.

It had taken just one week for the 18-year-old Jean Jessop, who said she had had no previous sexual experience, to become a London street-walker 'entertaining' hundreds of servicemen. Her wages rose from £1.10s per week to £12 per night with her change of career, but the job, as we shall see, was extremely dangerous.

AND THE END

Just a few months after Miss Jessop began her new job, Sarah Gwendoline Parry was touting for business in the Priory Tavern, North London. She was some twenty years older than Jean, but may well have started her 'national service' in the same way.

Sarah's last customer was Louis Walsh, a 37-

year-old electrician, whom the police medical officer later described as :

"A neurotic individual, inclined to be emotional and self-pitying, with the typical egotistic outlook of the neurotic."

Unfortunately, Louis did not have this government health warning pinned to his jacket. To Sarah, he was just another punter. Louis takes up the story in his confession to the police:

"While I was there I noticed two women sitting on chairs near where I was standing. One of the women glanced to me and smiled and talked to her friend in a voice loud enough for me to hear what she was saying, punctuating her conversation with glances and smiles in my direction. Clearly she wanted to attract my attention.

After a while the younger stood up and I sat down on her chair. The old woman then spoke to me, passing some general remark and we started to talk. She asked me to buy her a drink and a packet of cigarettes...

After a time she brought up the subject of sex, to which I offered no serious objection...After talking a little more the woman asked me if I had any money and I told her I had some money although actually I only had a few shillings. She then suggested I should go somewhere with her. I agreed and asked where we should go. She said, 'I can take you to a bombed house.'

When we got outside it was dark but we each had an electric torch. The woman took me to what appeared to be a large bombed house. We went into a room. From the feeling underfoot the floor seemed to be covered in a lot of rubble. From the light of a torch I saw an old-fashioned leather couch which had the guts torn out of it.

The woman sat down on the couch and said to me: 'What about the pound?' or words to that effect. I said: 'All right, you'll get it in good time' or something like that.

She said she wanted the money first and began to scream.

I clapped my hand over her mouth when she wouldn't stop and then with my right fist struck her a number of heavy blows about the face and head...

Finally she did become unconscious and I got up and shone my torch on her. I might have had the torch in my hand when I was striking her, but I don't remember."

Sir Bernard Spilsbury reported that most of the injuries were consistent with having been caused by severe blows with a fist. The injury on the left side of the neck, however, was caused by an instrument with a hard edge, possibly a torch.

Louis was adamant that when he left the battered woman she was still breathing. He quickly made his way back to the rented rooms he shared with his mother. Not knowing that Sarah was dead, he confessed to his landlady and asked if she had anything to remove bloodstains. He later burnt his clothes in the fireplace and disposed of the remains by flushing them down the lavatory. He could not keep his guilty secret from his mother, who, a few days later, read in the paper that a woman's body had been found in suspicious circumstances. Louis then made his third confession in the Roman Catholic church in Quex Road, Hampstead, and his fourth at the local police station.

With prostitutes being considered by many to be the lowest form of life, little sympathy was shown for the deceased. Both Louis' mother and landlady had referred to her as 'a bad woman'. The judiciary placed little value on Sarah's life, sentencing Louis Walsh to twenty-one months' imprisonment for manslaughter.

STRANGLED WITH A SILK STOCKING

A similar indifference to the fate of a prostitute was demonstrated the following year. The dead body of a streetwalker was discovered in a room near Victoria Station. She had been strangled with one of those much sought after silk stockings. There were signs of a struggle and police discovered fibres torn from the shirt of her assailant. These were quickly identified as coming from the same material issued to the U.S. Army Air Force. At least nine different sets of prints were taken from beer bottles and the wash basin. All the investigators now had to do was check the prints against the 4,000 or so American airmen who were off duty that day. Nine men were interviewed and all admitted to having had intercourse with the prostitute. Nobody would admit to the murder, and because of the uncertainty of the order in which the men visited the room, the case was taken no further. Reading between the lines, the prevalent attitude seems to have been, 'Why bother about the death of a cheap slut? We need these servicemen to fight the war.'

Not all servicemen resorted to prostitutes. Many fell in love with, and sometimes married, local girls. Unfortunately they did not always use their 'rubbers' or their brains and many girls were faced with the problem of unwanted pregnancies.

TWO LIVES WASTED

Arthur Wright made the following short statement on 20th August 1943.

1) Mary Evelyn Wright was my daughter aged 23. For the past three and a half years she has been employed as a lady cook at the Essex County Hospital, Colchester.

2) On 3rd July she came home from a holiday and left to go to London on July 5th.

3) On 8th July she returned home gravely ill and was under treatment by Dr. Cartledge until 19th July, when she was removed to the Grove Nursing Home, Norwich.

4) On the morning of 20th July I saw her dead body there.

Mary's three day stay in London had been in Sutton Court Road, Chiswick, where she had visited 59-year-old Jennie Barton, an abortionist. Like so many other girls, Mary had fallen for an American officer and was now three months pregnant. She met another Mary who recommended Jennie. But whereas one 'operation' went smoothly, the other resulted in the death of a young woman with her whole life before her.

Originally charged with manslaughter, Jennie Barton was eventually imprisoned for six months on the lesser charge of `using an instrument or other means to secure an abortion'. The evidence against her included:

1) Statement of accused dated 3rd August 1943.

2) Further statement of accused dated 5th August 1943.

3) Enema.

4) 'Bed and douche slipper.'

5) White enamel jug.

6) Partly used bottle of Lysol.

7) New bottle of Lysol.

8) Three full bottles of castor oil.

9) Two rubber sheets.

10) White enamel pail.

11) Three empty bottles.

The whole case came to light when the first Mary heard about the death of the second. She went immediately to the police and gave the following statement:

"In January 1943, I met an American officer, Captain Whittaker. I became very fond of him and intercourse took place between us. As a result I missed one of my periods in March this year. In the ordinary way I am very regular. I couldn't have a baby for family reasons and I made enquiries to find someone who could help me...I telephoned the accused to remind her I was coming on the following Friday. She told me to bring my clothes, some cotton wool and a packet of sanitary towels.

On the 11th June I arrived at the accused's house about 7.30 p.m....We then went to my bedroom. First she told me to undress and get into bed. I lay flat on my back. She appeared to massage my tummy with her left hand, she seemed to press down. She inserted her other hand into my front passage...After she had done this the accused left the room for a few minutes returning with an enema and an enamelled tin and gave me an enema in my front passage. She told me to remain in bed and to put on a sanitary towel. After the first treatment the accused said it was usual to settle the matter and I got my handbag and gave her £32....The pains got very bad and I sat down for a while. They got very bad and I asked the accused if I could go and lie down. I went up to bed, the accused coming with me. I got into bed and she examined my front passage, put her fingers up and said , ' It's there'. She left me to fetch a pail and told me to get up and sit on it, which I did. Something then came away from me and fell into the pail. The accused examined it. It came away completely in its bag. She said, 'It's a little boy' after she had opened the bag."

Mary Howard confided in Mary Wright and the latter arrived in Chiswick for the same operation about one month later. After firstly denying carrying out the botched abortion, Jennie Barton, in her second statement, gave a horrendous account of the torturous three days Mary Wright spent at her house, before being sent back to Norwich to die.

The newspapers of the times published hundreds of abortion stories. If a wife became pregnant by another man whilst her husband was stationed away, she did not have the possibility of adoption as permission from her husband was required by law. To conceal the pregnancy she might have moved to another part of the country and given birth. Most took the lonely road to the back-street abortionist.

When gaoled female abortionists were held in high esteem by their fellow prisoners.

OUT WITH THE OLD... IN WITH THE NEW

The advent of war was warmly greeted by one section of the population. Some 5,000 prisoners nearing the end of their sentences were discharged, and 2,000 moved. Borstal boys (ages 16-23), who had served not less than six months, were released, and the number of young offenders detained fell, at a stroke, from 2,500 to 800. Over the next few years there was to be a radical change in the make-up of the prison population. Where once professional lags spent their days sewing mailbags, a new, disciplined and principled category of prisoner emerged, posing the

65. Prisoners receiving weekly earnings and making small purchases of tobacco in Wandsworth. (Picture released July 1945).

authorities new and difficult problems.

Most of this new category had never been imprisoned before. They included those considered a threat to the state, either because of their political or religious beliefs, and those imprisoned simply because of their ethnic backgrounds. They were not prepared to do their time quietly, in the traditional manner.

Changes had to be effected because of the particular demands of wartime. With some 20% of prison officers being called up, there were not enough staff to safely supervise prison work. Consequently the prisoners toiled only five hours a day in the workshops, as opposed to the pre-war eight, although more work was done in the cells. Suddenly there developed a demand for all forms of labour and more than half the prisoner population became engaged in war work. Men were sent from Wormwood Scrubs to work on timber salvage sites at Hendon and Sunbury. Holloway, which had an average population of some 330 women, mostly serving sentences up to one month for offences like drunkenness, was emptied of most of its prisoners at the start of the war; those not being released were sent to continue their sentences at Aylesbury. Holloway was largely reserved for the detention of women arrested under regulation 18B, that is those 'prejudicial to the conduct of war.'

At first their numbers were small, but with the war going badly and the serious threat of invasion in May 1940, one of the first acts Churchill enforced was to inter all the Austrians and Germans living in Britain who might assist the enemy - this included all women aged between 16 and 60.

On 27th May, following a series of dawn raids in the capital, hundreds of women were roused from their beds and told to pack. Many had been living in London most of their lives. Even nurses were not spared, with one being led off to internment, leaving her patient in the bath. A German nun living in a closed convent was also uprooted and all excuses and protestations ignored. The arrested women hastily threw together as many clothes as they could squeeze into one suitcase and, along with children up to the age of 16, began their first experience of detention. A Times reporter observed that most of the women appeared to be under thirty and of the domestic-servant class. Those obviously wealthy appeared to be in the most distress. None knew what the future held.

66. Interned male aliens leaving for the Isle of Man, May 17th 1940.

67. Female aliens received early morning raids and were allowed to take one suitcase.

Only invalids, the infirm, the seriously ill or individuals in an advanced stage of pregnancy were exempted. Holloway was the destination for prisoners deemed most likely to assist the enemy, and their presence was much resented by some of the few 'genuine' experienced prisoners. This was how one of the `old lags' - as she called herself - described the situation to the Sunday Dispatch on 1st June 1940.

"The alien women, Germans, Austrians, some of them Jewesses, used to march around the exercise yard singing German songs, accompanied by mouth organs. The day I went into Holloway I was kept waiting from ten in the morning until ten at night while a big batch of them had their baggage examined before being allowed to take it into prison."

One of those waiting in the above queue may well have been Marie Neurath, who described the admissions procedure:

"At first we were put into little boxes like chicken boxes...We were allowed to use the toilet but had to keep the door open. Then we were stripped and investigated and given a bath and also a
toothbrush and a nightshirt. Then we were asked what our religion was and were given the appropriate forms of bible. Then we were taken to our cells - we each had separate cells."

Livia Laurent spent six weeks in Holloway before being transferred to the Isle of Man. She continued the story in her book 'A Tale of Internment':

"My cell was one of the 'sit down' ones in which you can neither stand, turn around or shake your head. There were some intriguing inscriptions on the walls, obviously put there by my new colleagues, the jail-birds.

'Off to Borstal now, he! he!' said one.

Another 'See you again chums; so long! I love Tom Taylor, you old hag.' and others which cannot be repeated but suggested entirely new possibilities."

Paradoxically, many of the internees had fled religious and political persecution in Germany and only had tenuous links with the Fatherland. They were now sharing a prison with British political prisoners who venerated Hitler. Livia observed these Germanophiles in the prison chapel on Sundays:

"Some of these English ladies were dressed in dirndls [a full skirt with a tight waistband] with long blonde plaits wound round their heads, German-fashion, clearly showing by their dress and behaviour where their sympathies were to be found...There were others in rich fox furs and small flower and fruit-laden hats carrying handbags and faultless white gloves, giving the impression they were patronising their parish church."

All of the prisoners prayed that they would not die alone in their cell during an air raid. Livia Laurent again:

"One night, I had just gone to bed and was reading aloud to myself when the sirens went . 'Click' the light was switched off, and I sat in darkness. For a moment I caught my breath. Would they keep us locked up during a raid? The droning of planes came near and anti-aircraft guns went into action. I dived into my slacks, put shoes and a coat on and sat on the bed, waiting, listening, shivering all over; please unlock me, please unlock me; I was frantic. Should I ring the bell, our only communication with the outside world? Usually it didn't help much. Either there were instructions to unlock us, or we would stay where we were, each one alone in a cell, helpless and frightened while the Battle of Britain was raging outside.

Someone did ring a bell. It sounded thin and pathetic against the bangs without. But it was a signal. Everybody started ringing bells, banging on doors, knocking at walls, shouting, screaming.

'Unlock us, unlock us, let us out, let us out, help, hurry.' The uproar was terrific. The call was repeated in other wings until the whole prison resounded with bells ringing, feet stamping, chairs being hurled against doors and frightened women screaming at the top of their voices: 'Let us out.' The chattering of keys was heard now, and hurriedly one door after another was opened by the wardresses in dressing gowns flashing their torches into each cell."

The prisoners, desperate for human contact as they heard the bombs exploding all around, gathered in one cell to bolster each other's spirits until the merciful, welcoming sound of the all clear.

Most alien prisoners were sent to the Isle of Man, but this did not free prisons from being directly involved in the war effort. Wardens eventually had to deal with a number of differing categories of prisoners. One of these was the conscientious objector.

68. Holloway prison. Women internees sat alone petrified and prayed in their cells as the bombs fell.

SCENES FROM THE CONCHIE COURT

The Government had learnt a lot from their heavy handling of `conchies' in the First World War and prison sentences were only prescribed when an objector blatantly refused to do any work which might help the war effort, accordingly only 1% of them were gaoled. Tribunals to determine the validity of an objector's beliefs were set up and their findings widely reported in the newspapers.

In 1940 the South London Press published a series of articles under the headline; 'From the Conchie Court.' Here they reported on the complicated discussions taking place between objectors and a determined team of interrogators. John Reed, a flower-seller from Peckham, was a Buddhist who practised yoga. He argued that joining the army would 'upset his life of harmony in the universe and his progress spiritually.' The tribunal argued that Buddhists were fighting for China against Japan and refused exemption.

Another objector argued, "I would suffer complete moral degradation and serious consequences in the hereafter if I broke the covenant with God."

With the later conscription of women for war work, the occasional female came before the board. Ruby Humphreys could not find the time to do war work at Holloway Sanatorium. She argued, 'My time is fully occupied in my work as a Christian Evangelist and social worker in harmony with my consecration to Almighty God.' Refusing to pay the £5 fine, Ruby was jailed for one month.

Other objectors were not quite so eloquent but no less sincere. Thomas Dammery, a Southern Railway carriage cleaner simply said: 'Killing people does no good to them.'

Some conscientious objectors were imprisoned in Wormwood Scrubs. Sidney Grays recalls that prisoners serving sentences for robbery with violence were better treated than those refusing to help the war effort. He, too, remembers the sheer naked terror evoked by the sound of the siren:

"I remember during air-raids there was panic in the prison because we were all locked up. If the prison were hit there was no way you could get out. Prisoners would bang plates, jerries, mugs, anything; it was an enormous noise."

With only one in a hundred objectors ending up in prison, the number of conchies being detained at the end of the war had become insignificant.

THE NEW ORDER

With the threat of invasion diminishing, and the transfer of aliens to the Isle of Man, prisons in the capital in 1941 did have some spare capacity. With the growing number of 'new' crimes, however, cells were quickly reoccupied. The burgeoning black market and the blackout tempted many otherwise honest citizens into breaking the law, some of whom were sent directly to gaol. Moreover, with the influx of foreign soldiers, brothel-keeping offences increased and the prison population was further swollen by serving soldiers sentenced by courts martial. Meanwhile, crime in the form of burglary, shop-lifting, fraud and assault did not stop just because there was a war on. This combination of old and new crime meant that the overall prison population increased during the war years.

Juvenile offences also increased. Many youngsters new to crime were apprehended. Their

69. Holloway prison again. A surrealistic scene with inmates dancing in their heavy shoes.

70. None of the prisoners on A wing were allowed to eat in the dining hall. They were described as 'dirty in habit, appearance and cleaning of cells'.

offences were directly attributed to conditions caused by air raids, the destruction of schools, the loss of homes and the uncontrolled existence of living between shelters and ruined streets. With fathers and elder brothers away, mothers and elder sisters working or queuing for rations, the devil made work.

But it was not only young people who were offending more, there was also a steep rise in the number of prosecutions of women for shop-lifting - especially clothes - and for the neglect of children, an offence often caused by the long hours of war work and increased food shortages. The female prison population doubled during the six years of war and the combined daily average prison population in England and Wales rose from around 10,000 in 1939 to nearly 15,000 in 1945.

Some people thought prison was the safest place to be during the war and, indeed, despite several bombs landing on or near London's gaols - Pentonville was extensively damaged in 1941 - no staff or inmates were killed as the result of enemy bombing. Prisons had their own 'fire-squad' to help deal with incendiary devices. Inmates were

entitled to the same rations as the general public and most spent some time working to help the war effort. On the whole, therefore, life inside was not too bad. But just as risks were minimal, so were opportunities. No escapes were effected as an indirect result of enemy action.

LIFE ON THE INSIDE

But what was it like for the prison officers? Miss H spent four months doing the job in Holloway in 1944. She qualified in just one day after a perfunctory medical and was employed at the rate of eight shillings per day plus 2s 6d war bonus. From the very first she hated the job and was not overly impressed by her fellow workers:

"The majority of the regular officers are extremely dull, mentally and physically. There is little or no comradeship even among the younger ones and they are always trying to catch each other out. They are jealous of each other...Every officer is as unpleasant as possible towards colleagues but even more so towards prisoners."

Miss H was given advice by one of the more experienced officers:

"They'll lead you a 'ell of a life if you don't treat them like they are - animals - that's what they're in here for."

The new recruit was once admonished before both prisoners and officers alike for appearing too happy in her work:

"Miss H don't you know you're here to stop the prisoners from whistling and singing, don't you think you should set an example?"

Some regulations were extremely petty. If an inmate had almost reached the top of a flight of stairs and an officer wished to descend, the prisoner would almost inevitably be ordered to the bottom. Most officers accepted bribes and for a sum of money - usually ten times the 'outside' price - would smuggle in cigarettes or sweets or occasionally liquor. Sometimes prisoners would hand over a large sum, about £10, and ask for it all to be spent on cosmetics. If other officers detected the smuggling, they would denounce their fellow worker and then take her place in the supply chain. The most popular newspaper was the News of the World, much sought after so prisoners could see which of their friends had 'been done' and what the new arrivals were in for.

Inmates wore woollen stockings and cotton dresses with one layer of flannelette underwear and navy blue serge coats, which had become thin through over-use and too much washing. Initially, the laundry workers would wash and iron both prisoners' and officers' clothes, but when the underwear of unpopular officers was returned in rags, the laundering of officers' clothes was discontinued. Inmates constantly complained about the cold.

Work hours were from 10-12 and 2-4, when inmates were returned to their cells, served tea and locked up for the night. The distribution of the midday meal often led to heated exchanges. Most of the prisoners working in the kitchens were Borstal girls under 21, who were more spirited than the old lags and would often steal their dinners. They knew that because of their age they could not be severely punished. Many prisoners would sell their dinner or pudding (on the three days a week when pudding was served) for a 'short' cigarette or even a dog-end. Full-length cigarettes were broken into four to make them last.

Cells were inspected whilst prisoners worked and if not spotlessly clean, a notice would be chalked on the offending place, e.g. 'this floor must be scrubbed'.

None of the prisoners in A wing were allowed to leave their cells to work. These were women suffering from V.D., scabies or lice and described by Miss H as, 'dirty in habit, appearance and cleaning of cells.' They would sit in the doorway and sew sacks and were only allowed out to see the doctor, fetch water or empty slops.

There were the usual unofficial categories of 'acceptable' and 'unacceptable' crime. Those most despised were the women imprisoned for petty pilfering or neglecting their children.

One mother, imprisoned for a month, was particularly reviled by her new neighbours. Emily was charged with wilfully neglecting her four sons and one daughter, aged 14,9,7,5 and 2 years respectively. The 40-year-old Stepney woman pleaded guilty. A police surgeon testified that the home was very dirty, the mattresses being filthy with a heap of old clothes being used as bedding. The children were verminous and suffering from scabies and sores on their bodies and legs. Emily was barely able to cope, as is evidenced by her words as she scolded her children in the presence of a police officer:

"Behave yourself, if you don't they will take you away - I do not care very much if they do."

When faced with the prospect of leaving one form of imprisonment for another, Emily threatened to commit suicide rather than endure the harassment of 30 days in Holloway.

In the prison hierarchy drug addicts were considered to be higher than the majority of prisoners, but the most admired women were the abortionists. An abortion even took place in Holloway, performed by one prisoner on another, without the authorities being any the wiser. On Saturday afternoons, there being no work, the prisoners were allowed to sit in their cells with the doors open. This was the only possible time that the 'operation' could take place. A quantity of Dettol was stolen from the hospital and secreted, probably in the toilet. The termination was crudely effected with just the disinfectant, hot water and an ordinary bone toothbrush. The patient duly asked to see the doctor, complained that she had had a miscarriage and was subsequently excused work for a few days.

Being confined to cells eighteen hours out of twenty-four led to the odd 'smashing-up' fit. Women would break anything breakable, tear anything tearable, beat on anything beatable and scream for attention. If the prisoner was in a cell more than one hundred years old there was a hole, especially designed, through which a water-hose could be inserted and its contents played on the prisoner to cool her down. In more modern cells the door had to be opened before the cold shower could be administered, providing opportunities for gratuitous violence.

On one occasion, several young prisoners barricaded themselves in one cell blocking the door with mattresses. Two male engineers trained the hoses on them whilst others removed the lock from the door. Once entry had been gained, fifteen women officers, about four for each prisoner, took over. The girls were told to strip and put on the nightdresses provided. If they offered any physical resistance they were laid into with shoes and keys and fists. Thus attired, they were then dragged by their hair down three flights of iron stairs and thrust into a bare cell with a stone floor. The two engineers then re-appeared and played hoses on them until the wretched girls' screams died away into sobs. They were only given dry clothing when officers were sure they would no longer put up a fight. In punishment cells, beds, mattresses and blankets were put in only at night, but if prisoners needed to use the lavatory they could do so only at the discretion of the officer on duty.

Women refusing to work received the same treatment as those above. One beating with shoes was only terminated following the intervention of one of the officers:

"I think she's had enough girls, leave her alone, poor bitch!"

Regulations governing the 'goodnight check' involved the officer saying 'All right?' to each of the 300 prisoners. The expected reply was 'Yes. Goodnight, Miss.' If this was not forthcoming the relevant cell had to be unlocked to make sure the prisoner was still alive. After her first evening shift Miss H left the prison and said to the gatekeeper: 'After all those goodnights if you expect me to say goodnight to you - you're crazy!'

Miss H said her final goodbye, or more probably her good riddance, to Holloway in January 1945.

THE WELCOME HOME

71. Soldiers and sailors in the building trade demobbed in November 1945. They are leaving Olympia with their clothing in boxes. Many had trouble adapting to civilian life.

72. *Because of the passage of time and effects of hard work, wives may not have been as pretty as their husbands remembered them.*

'HELLO STRANGER'

After long years of separation, many husbands and wives experienced severe difficulties readapting to life together. Both were likely to have undergone a serious change of character because of their wartime experiences.

Men had lost dear friends and comrades on the battlefield. Those who had spent years away retained an idealised memory of family life, forgetting the drudgery of domestic chores, the difficulties of having to scrimp and save to make ends meet. Because of the passage of time and effects of hard work, their wives and girlfriends may not have been as pretty as they remembered them. Children had grown up and barely recognised their fathers, who duly felt alienated, strangers in their own homes. Some even returned to find additions to the family, unaccountable cuckoos in the nest whom they had never been told about.

Moreover, life in civvy street was controlled by those who, for one reason or another, had never been to war. Greeted by slick spivs, who loitered round army camps, offering big money for de-mob suits, servicemen began to question why they'd fought at all. Returnees soon became depressed, jealous and resentful. Many also felt restless. In the army all their needs had been met; now they were confronted by the shortages and rationing civilians had long endured. Many lost weight.

The W.V.S. anticipated these problems in a newsletter in 1945:

"The returned men are going to find it very difficult to adjust to home life again. They have grown used to getting their food in pretty good quantity; now they will have to witness the shopping, the queuing, the contriving with rations that their wives must put into each meal."

Some servicemen had been educated by the war. After seeing the splendour of Italian architecture, for example, it was difficult to re-adapt to life in the London slums. Others were deeply affected by wartime experiences both on and off the battlefield. Although not fully appreciated at the time, many also suffered from the classic symptoms of Post Traumatic Stress Disorder: flashbacks, nightmares, nightsweats, panic, fits of uncontrollable violence and feelings of disorientation.

Civilian women had also changed. Three-quarters of married women were working by the end of the war. They had broken into jobs ranging from street

73. The cautious kiss. Husbands and wives had changed during the long separations. Domestic problems usually began some two months after demobilisation.

cleaning to banking, which had previously been male domains. Not only did they have to put in long hours, on the buses or in factories for example, they also had to keep their homes running and their children fed. This entailed hours of queuing, at several different shops, for meagre rations. Sleep was often interrupted by air raids. Over time, many women became envious of their husbands, who did not have to make decisions, were on better rations and had the time to write romanticised letters home, from what appeared to be exotic locations. In short, by the end of the war many women had been bombed out, blacked out and burnt out.

The men had their usual double standards. They saw it as perfectly acceptable to fraternise with local girls wherever they were posted - at home or abroad. They expected, however, that their wives remain loyal and chaste. Many had married in haste and spent very little time with their wives, who found the separation particularly difficult. A probation officer reported why some women sought out new partners:

"Many excellent young mothers have been unable to stand the loneliness at home, particularly when their husbands are abroad, with not even spasmodic leave to break the monotony...Hasty war marriages, on embarkation leave, sometimes between comparative strangers, within a few days or weeks of married life, have left both parties with little sense of responsibility or obligation towards each other."

Many servicemen were terrified of who their wives may have been seeing during their absences. They were particularly concerned about what the Americans may have been getting up to. Their worries were reinforced when books like 'More Gum Chum' appeared on the market. It contained 34 cartoons about how British girls and married women were getting on - or getting off? - with American servicemen.

Those married women who did their bit to entertain foreign troops ran a far greater risk than any unfaithful husband. They were playing at home while he was playing away. There was no home advantage - the spectators were only too willing to pass on a copy of the fixture list to returning husbands.

Marital breakdown tended to occur 2-4 months after a husband was demobbed. Sometimes it did not take that long. Sergeant Cairns returned from Italy to his home in Staines in 1946. When his wife told him she intended to leave him, he whipped out his pistol and shot her between the eyes. He then turned the gun on himself and fired a bullet into the back of his head. He died instantly.

'SHE LOVES HER HUSBAND A LITTLE MORE.'

Not all returning servicemen were dumped by wives who had taken temporary lovers. Evacuated to Wales, in 1943, Violet Holloway's husband had been overseas for some time, when she met and fell in love with Raymond Rees. Despite his parents' objections to his teaming up with a married woman, the couple set up home together in Stepney. With the end of the war and imminent return of her husband, Violet told the Welshman to follow the example of Norman Tebbit's father.

Raymond wrote a letter to his parents about the end of the affair. They were so worried by the contents that they immediately contacted the police. When questioned at Old Street Police Station, the 27-year-old process worker said:

"I wrote that if I could not have her I was going to make sure that no other man would have her. You see I am madly in love with her...Now that her husband has come back from the army she has gone back to him...she has told me that she loves me but she loves her husband a little more."

Raymond was charged at the Old Bailey with sending a letter threatening to murder a married woman. Following his plea of guilty, the letter was read out in court:

"Well, ma, yesterday I decided to kill Vi. I know it is hard for you to believe that I could do such a thing but I could. There is only one thing stopping me, ma. I have caused you enough worry in your life.

I feel like killing him because I don't want her to be with him."

It was revealed in court that Raymond made suicide threats after Violet reneged on promises to obtain a divorce. The wronged husband had meanwhile returned and forgiven her and was back in Germany, by August 1945, when the case came to court.

After spending one month in Brixton Prison the infatuated Welshman was bound over for three years and sent back to his parents in Wales. Clearly he'd used his time on remand for reflection. At his trial he acknowledged the end of the affair with these words:

"I have changed my mind now and will leave her alone."

'WHAT THE EYE DOESN'T SEE.'

Some things are best left unsaid. We can only hope that the anonymous writer of a letter addressed to Violet Williams' Fulham home never learnt of the tragic consequences of this act.

Evan Williams had rejoined the navy during the war and spent three years in the United States. He co-habited with an American woman for much of his stay there, but at the end of hostilities returned to his family home on 1st September 1945.

His 42-year-old wife appeared very cold and distant and he soon found out why. She told him that she had received a letter from America informing her that he had been associating with a woman there. Evan, following his sojourn in the States, could not tell a lie. Violet's worst fears were confirmed.

Three and a half weeks later, Evan found his wife lying in the kitchen, her head in the gas oven. She was unconscious but after hastily applying artificial respiration he managed to revive her. Evan confided in his daughter about the suicide attempt but did not inform the doctor as he wanted to keep the affair within the family.

From that day on the daughter locked the kitchen door every night so her mother could not get to the stove. Five days later the daughter saw her mother undress and get into bed at 11.30. p.m. The daughter awoke at eight and wondered why her mother had not called her, as was her custom, at 6.30. a.m. She went to her room and found that the bed had been slept in. Going down to the basement she saw her mother through the window outside the house. She was wearing her nightdress and slippers. She was also dangling from a rope. Some 16 feet in length it had been secured to a railing outside the bedroom window.

On the under part of the nightdress a letter was pinned. It was not read out in court.

74. Women took over the jobs vacated by men at the front. (1940).

MURDER IN THE DARK

75. *"It appeared that the dress had been deliberately arranged."*

"I saw the body of a woman. She was lying with her feet pointing towards Grenade Street. Her arms were outstretched and she appeared lifeless. The dress was folded back on to her stomach just above the pubic hair. It was a neat fold as if it had been arranged. There were no signs of violence on the body, except for scratches at the neck and there were no signs on the ground around the body."

Inspector John Rowe had been summoned to Rich Street, E.14. early in the morning of 6th. August 1945. Shortly after 5.a.m. the body of 27-year-old Lilian Hartney had been discovered by a stableman on his way to the dairy. The dead woman wore neither stockings nor panties.

One of the Inspector's colleagues noticed small marks and indentations on the wrist and commented about the position of the corpse:

"It appeared that the body and dress had been deliberately arranged."

The doctor arrived by six and, because both the upper parts of the body and chest beneath the clothing were still warm, suggested Lilian had been dead between six and seven hours. Post-mortem rigidity had begun in the exposed arms and neck but had not descended to the lower limbs.

There were signs of strangulation.

The body was sent to the pathologist, who made his usual thorough examination. Bite marks were found around both nipples with the nature of the wounds indicating that the biter had two teeth in the lower jaw missing. Pressure marks were discovered on the victim and these were consistent with Lilian having had both forearms tied with a stout cord.

Scratch marks were noted on the forearms, hands and right thigh, but there was no evidence of recent sexual intercourse. Both the bite and rope marks had been inflicted before death. Because of the pattern of bruising, the assault had probably occurred on a soft surface, such as a bed, and not on the hard pavement where she was found. To counter this there was no evidence that the body had been dragged or pulled along.

The cause of death was asphyxia due to manual strangulation. The pathologist noted at the post-mortem that the bladder was empty, this being common in asphyxial death although no traces of urine were found near the body and none on the victim's clothes.

An inspector had recognised the body as Mrs Hartney and the police prepared themselves for the thankless task of breaking the news to the deceased woman's husband. Patrick and Lilian Hartney had lived together in an unkempt, second floor bed-sitter some 250 yards from the side street in which Lilian's body had been found. The house, at 32, East India Dock Road, was made up of ten rooms, nine of which were let to various tenants. Patrick was found in one of the back rooms. When the officers arrived he was discovered lying on a double-bed, the bed-clothes pulled up to his shoulders. They were surprised to find the ex-stoker dressed and in his first statement, he confirmed that he had been lying in bed fully clothed and had not changed for about two weeks. One policeman observed that Hartney's trousers were well-pressed and not crumpled, as would have been the case had he slept in them. One half of the double bed had not been slept in.

Patrick told the police that his wife had gone out the previous evening and had not yet returned. He added:

'She has been highly strung and sometimes she gets bad-tempered and goes off.'

After being informed that Lilian had met with a nasty accident, Hartney was escorted the short distance to Rich Street and en route informed that his wife had been murdered. The police were later surprised at how quickly he identified the body of his wife. Although a tarpaulin covered much of the dead woman's face, her husband casually pronounced: `That's her.'

Quite why Lilian married a man twice her age is not known, although there is strong evidence that she wed the recently discharged chief petty-officer on the rebound. Patrick, who had tuberculosis, met Lilian, then working as a cleaner, in 1940 and married her four years later; he was 50 and she 26. Just before the marriage she had written to him saying she was in love with another man, but a few weeks later was reconciled with Patrick. When questioned about his marriage, the ex-sailor admitted that his wife was not happy, complaining she was 'fed up'.

According to Patrick, Lilian was highly-sexed and enjoyed having her breasts bitten and sucked and needed sex every day. He said that Lilian was in the habit of not wearing knickers if there were no clean ones available and had not worn stockings for several weeks.

76. Lilian Hartney's strangled body was found some 250 yards from her home.

Patrick Hartney confided in Police Sergeant Stonehouse, who made the following notes:

"She told me last Saturday night I was no good to her...She wanted a man every night. She liked you to lay on top of her for half an hour after you had finished and bite her breasts and neck. I could not do it with my complaint. That is why she used to be fed up with me."

With some 50% of murdered women being killed

77. The Hartneys lived in a back room of the second house from the left on the East India Dock Road.

by their husbands or ex-partners, Patrick was the logical suspect and police began a detailed search of the musty bed-sitter. A copy of Mrs. Belloc Lowndes murder story 'The Lodger' was found open on the page where Lilian had last put it down. Of more interest to the searchers were the two sheets, both of which were badly stained by urine. On one of the sheets, which had been dried by the gas fire, a stain measured 14" by 22". When questioned as to how the sheets had come to be in this condition, Patrick replied that his wife had "wetted the bed" some four days previously. (Lilian's mother later denied that her daughter had ever been a bed-wetter). A detective felt under the second soiled sheet on the bed and found the mattress dry, but when he turned it over a substantial damp patch was discovered. The remains of burnt cord, exactly the same type and size (one eighth of an inch) as was used to bind the victim, were found in the grate. Patrick, who had been sweating profusely since the policemen's

arrival, knew what must have been going through their minds. He protested his innocence in a manner virtually guaranteed to implicate himself:

"I did not murder my wife. I did not kill her. We bought some fish and plums and she cooked them, but got up from dinner and went on the bed and would not clear up the table. She would not do a thing for me. If they say they heard screams in the house that night it is lies, because she did not come home that night."

The police believed that Patrick murdered his wife, possibly after she had taunted him about his sexual inadequacy, and dumped the body in the early hours of the morning. In the absence of further information, however, this was only a theory. Indeed, they told the press that whilst they knew the identity of the killer they were mystified as to the motive.

Patrick had two teeth missing from his lower jaw,

which tied in with the marks left on the dead woman's body, and this, together with the evidence of the cord and urine stains, prompted them to arrest the seaman. Hartney strenuously denied his guilt but otherwise invoked his right of silence. Samples of trace evidence were taken from the suspect's nails, which were long and... *"had not been cut for some time but gave the impression of having recently been cleaned."*

For the whole six months from the murder to the trial, Patrick protested his innocence. In this he was supported by a neighbour, Isabella Fairey, with whom he talked immediately after his first police interview:

"They are trying to pin something on me because I was already dressed when the police came in."

He went on to give the opinion that his wife was better off where she was.

Isabella was impressed by how ill, weak and 'incapable of physical violence' Hartney appeared to be.

After his arrest, it became obvious, during questioning, that Patrick disapproved of his wife staying out all night:

"She has been getting around Chinatown. I couldn't do anything with her."

This remark provided the police with evidence of motive.

After several months of deteriorating health, Patrick Hartney stood trial for the murder of his wife at the Central Criminal Court on February 2, 1946. Because of the advanced state of his tuberculosis, a doctor, the senior medical officer at Brixton Prison, was present for every day of Patrick's trial. The prosecution suggested that Patrick had strangled his wife in their bed-sit and then dumped her body in the early hours of the morning.

The jury attentively assessed the medical evidence.

Lilian's throat had been messily covered with nail marks, scratches and abrasions. Two bruises, each half an inch in diameter, were found in the muscles over the voice box. The pathologist believed that a first attempt at strangulation was unsuccessful. Details of the bite marks on the breasts and absence of urine where the body was discovered were also pointed out.

Sarah Koffmann, the landlady, testified that she saw Mrs. Hartney leave the house at about 8 o'clock on the Saturday evening, 4th August, and return early on the Sunday morning. John Brophy, who rented a room in the same house, confirmed

that he had let Lilian in at about 8. a.m. and had previously done so once or twice on Sunday mornings.

Later on that Sunday Isabella Fairey saw the Hartneys in their room. Patrick had been sitting up against the door while Lilian prepared tea. He had apologised for the untidy state of the room. Fairey added:

"They were not quarrelling but they appeared to be sulky."

Lilian went to Isabella's room until 8. p.m. on the

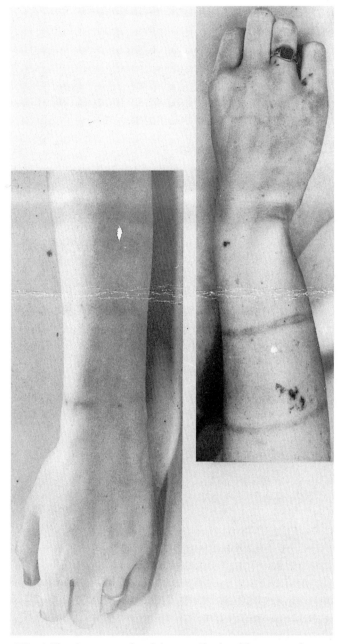

78. Lilian's arms had been tied with a cord one eighth of an inch thick. Cord the same size was found in the couple's bedsitter.

Sunday evening, when Patrick called her upstairs. She went up for a moment and then left the house. She visited a neighbouring couple for about an hour and the only person to see her after that was her killer.

Another neighbour, Mrs. Lilian Morgan, reported

being awakened by shuffling outside her room and that she'd later heard a noise in the backyard.

D.I. John Freshey confirmed that he had examined the house on the morning the body was discovered and found that cobwebs on the back door had been broken, indicating that the door had recently been opened.

Prosecuting counsel contested that:

"Hartney tied up his wife, partly strangled her, she partly recovered and he finally killed her, then carried her to the spot where she was finally found."

The time had come for the enfeebled suspect to be cross-examined. Patrick Hartney in the witness box declared:

"I loved my wife. I had no other relative in the world beside her. I did not murder her."

Mr. Anthony Hawke (prosecuting): *"Are you really telling the jury that in the middle of August you found you could sleep better at night by wearing your shirt and trousers and socks?"*

Hartney: *"Yes."*

Mr. Hawke: *"Or is the fact you were found like that by the police more consistent with your returning in the early hours of the morning after a most exhausting journey and having only the energy to take your collar and tie and shoes off, and throw yourself on the bed."*

Here the Judge intervened: *"That is a matter for the jury."*

"Was your wife taunting you with the fact that you were deteriorating physically?"

"She used to say I was no good to her."

"Was she taunting you with it?"

"Yes."

"Was it preying on your mind?"

"It may have to a certain extent."

Contrary to an earlier statement, Patrick denied ever having bitten his wife.

The prosecution seemed to have a strong case. There was the evidence of the soiled sheets and burnt cord found at the couple's bedsitter; the defendant had been discovered dressed and perspiring; the teeth marks around the nipples showed similarities to Hartney's bite; the testimony of the neighbours and the broken cobwebs on the back door all pointed one way. The sole argument the defence made concerned the physical ability of Patrick Hartney to lug his wife's dead weight over 250 yards. Mr. Lawton, defending, simply asked the jury if they thought a man in the defendant's enfeebled state could carry his wife, nearly a stone heavier than himself, to the place where the body was discovered.

The jury deliberated for two hours at the end of the two week trial.

"Do you find the defendant, Patrick Hartney, guilty or not guilty of murder?"

"Not guilty."

Patrick was released at 6.20. p.m. and was immediately congratulated by his friends. He stated that he had never doubted that the jury would set him free:

"It has been simply terrible waiting all these months with this awful thing hanging over me."

He probably never saw the police medical officer's report:

"As to his physical condition, I have no doubt that his period of life will be short."

It is not known when Patrick Hartney died. The Metropolitan Police files on the case are closed until the year 2024.

79. Many took the opportunites presented by wartime conditions to leave their old lives behind. There was a thriving market for stolen or forged ration books and identity cards.

UNDER COVER OF THE NIGHT

80. Deaths on the road almost trebled during the black-out. The most dangerous time to be wandering the streets was between 10 and 11pm in December. Adult pedestrians were at the greatest risk followed by drivers of motor vehicles.

In Manchester, as in London, the whole way of life and nature of crime changed in wartime conditions. Emergency local regulations were passed to combat all possible dangers. Two poisonous snakes in Belle Vue Gardens were to be shot as soon as the first air raid occurred in any part of the country. The grounds were patrolled by armed officials with orders to fire if any dangerous animals escaped.

The air raids led to a whole cross section of the population, who would not normally have mixed, spending hours in cramped shelters in a zoo-like atmosphere. For the most part the overcrowding and unhygienic conditions were tolerated but, on occasions, especially at weekends when the pubs turned out, there was a degree of rowdyism as bands of young hooligans sang bawdy songs and swore - both at, and like - troopers. Some, who insisted on playing accordions and mouth organs were not always in tune with the wishes of other shelter seekers.

Domestic quarrels caused through drunkenness often erupted as dirty washing was aired in public places. Some of the more sensitive inhabitants risked the bombing and took to the streets to escape the squalor in the less harmonious shelters. In September, 1940, a man and his wife ran nearly two miles through the streets of Manchester as bombs exploded all around. In the first shelter they stumbled upon they found a drunken married couple swearing and squaring up to each other. In another two men were actually fighting and the police had been called in. In a third, conditions were 'perfectly beastly' owing to the unceasing foul language and numbers of men and women retching up. Indeed it was mooted by those passing bylaws that rowdy behaviour should lead to expulsion.

During raids some actually tempted fate by wandering the streets on sightseeing sorties. One warden particularly objected to the young women who popped into his shelter:

81. *The accident rate was so high that major campaigns were needed to warn both drivers and pedestrians of the danger of driving without lights in unlit streets.*

"Many of them insisted on going out into the street and staggering about to see what is happening, and of course, we are in danger when we try to get them back."

In one particularly heavy bombing raid just before Christmas, 1940, 396 people, perhaps including some of the inquisitive girls, lost their lives and over one thousand were injured.

It was not just the bombing that resulted in civilian deaths, the carnage on the roads, caused by the black-out, was a national disgrace. In the last four months of 1938 there were 37 recorded fatal road accidents in Manchester, the following year, for the same period, the figure had risen to 93 - the majority being adult pedestrians. Most fatalities were recorded in December between 10 and 11. p.m.

One unexpected result of the ban on lighting was the increase in the number of men who took the opportunity to live out their fantasies by dressing as women and wandering the streets after dark. When arrested for gross indecency, the transvestites would be photographed in both male and female attire. One unknown warrior was taken to the station clad in what at first seemed to be a full samurai rig-out.

The black-out conditions and mayhem caused by bombing were a godsend to another small but significant portion of the population; the criminal fraternity.

With the high demand fuelled by the black market, housebreaking, shopbreaking and warehouse raids increased dramatically throughout the war as detection rates plummeted. Manchester's clear up rate was amongst the worst in the country dropping from two in three offences being detected in 1942 to less than one in three by 1945. Manchester was particularly targeted by professional thieves because of its largish number of textile warehouses.

The figures for the value of goods stolen were even more alarming and showed a ten fold increase from £26,000 in 1938 to £260,000 in 1946. 21-year-old Gabrielle Rutherford was a typical opportunist thief whose modus operandi was simplicity itself. She told Manchester City Police Court in September, 1943:

"I used to choose a house with a door open. I would walk in, and if I saw a handbag or anything I would take it"

Charged with stealing clothing and other articles worth £13 from a house in Chorlton-on-Medlock, the homeless young woman asked for an astonishing 68 cases of larceny, housebreaking and forgery to be taken into consideration. The state insisted they look after her accommodation and nutritional needs for the next twelve months.

Children too got into the act. Whereas there were 487 recorded juvenile crimes in Manchester in 1934 the figure rose to 1,241 in 1940. Most were charged with breaking into shops and houses. There was also a marked increase in the theft of motor vehicles and the term 'joyriding' was surprisingly in use as long ago as 1940.

Many determined to help themselves rather than their country. Experienced and novice shoplifters alike made for department stores such as Lewis's.

Nine of the first ten shoplifters apprehended (below) in 1940 were female. There was no real pattern but torches and stockings were high on every thief's 'shopping' list. A register of further goods liberated, along with their prices, would suggest that nothing was safe from the light-fingered wartime shoppers. Shoplifters were apprehended trying to smuggle out: hot crab paste (6d) 1 pixie hat (4s. 11d) a jar of lime curd (6d) one box of Nestle Easter eggs (3s) three balls of wool (1s. 10d) a gas mask container (5s) 4 tins of milk of magnesia tablets (4s) a two-piece suit (£3.13s. 6d) 2 balloons (3d) 3 rubber gloves (1s 3d) 1 hornby train (14s) an Indian outfit (17s) and yes, the cuddly toy - a teddy bear - and for the thief with a conscience, a rosary.

The total value of goods stolen in 1940 was £273. 12s. The store prosecuted in nearly every case and an 11-year-old boy was dispatched to a remand home for 28 days for stealing two books. A persistent young offender of the same age was sent to approved school for three years. Mercy was shown in just one case when the perpetrator was heavily pregnant.

By 1943 shoplifting in Manchester was at twice the prewar levels. A police official explained that this was due to three reasons: clothes rationing, the ban on wrapping paper and a shortage of supervisory staff. A stores manager was at his wits end:

'On busy days we estimate that we have 40 or 50 people in the shop to every one assistant... our losses are enormous and going up week by week.'

DETAILS OF SHOPLIFTING OFFENCES FROM LEWIS'S, MARKET STREET, MANCHESTER IN 1940

GOODS STOLEN	VALUE	AGE	PUNISHMENT
Ladies shoes	9s.6d.	41	fined 20s.
Gloves, handkerchief, scarf	15s. 9d.	61	bound over to pay costs
2 camis, 1 vest, 1 pr. knickers 1 pr. gents gauntlets ankle socks, 4 prs. stockings pixie scarf, 2 prs. shoes soap	£3 1s. 11d.	36	12 months probation
2 vests, 2prs. pyjamas 4 prs. socks, 1 pr. braces 3 lighters, 1 pr. gloves 2 scarves	£8.16s. 8d.	50	4 months in prison
1 pr. strollers 4 prs. shoes	£1.19. 8d.	18	12 months probation
1 pr. shoes 1 table cloth	15s. 2d.	33	12 months probation
Shoes, stockings, pillow slips, fountain pen	£1 10s 0d.	14	2 months probation
2 prs. stockings, make up, handkerchiefs	19s. 8d	14	12 months probation
Necklace, powder puff, scarf, compact etc	£1.13s. 4d.	60	fined 40s.

It was not just the light fingered who troubled the store detectives. Many of the shops' staff were dismissed for defrauding their employers by ringing up bills of 9d instead of 3s. 9d when their friends presented their shopping, and by deliberately not charging for meals etc. Shoppers, too, had to be ever vigilant in queues as handbags were snatched, principally for the precious ration books.

Many previously honest people gave into temptation in the extraordinary times. Even the police took the opportunities presented by the wartime conditions to liberate goods. 31-year-old P.C. Thomas Parry of Crumpsall knew the value of ladies stockings. When investigating a theft from a shop in Oxford road he surreptitiously raised his steel helmet and deftly smuggled in three pair - value 11s. 9d. Daydreaming about the treats that may lay in store for him that evening when he presented the stolen stockings to his wife, he was rudely brought back to earth by a suspicious Inspector Ireland who ordered that he be searched at the police station.

After appearing astonished and asking 'How did they get there?' Parry knew the game was up and confessed: 'I took them on the spur of the moment. I am only a probationer. I hope you will not be too hard on me.' Parry was sent to gaol for two months and dismissed from the force.

THE GADABOUT GIRLS

As in London, prostitution flourished in Manchester in the war years, especially after the arrival of American servicemen. There was little else for the G.I.s to do when on leave as they did not particularly take to the city. The U.S. Consul George Armstrong wrote in July, 1942:

'Manchester has the appearance of a very grim town...it is particularly lonely on Sundays when the soldiers come in.'

Demetrius Tratolos of Whalley Range did his best to bring a little entertainment to the rich visitors from across the pond. He transformed his home into a club with all life's forbidden pleasures available...at a price. After observing several men and women arriving sober, and later leaving somewhat the worse for wear, the police determined to smash this illegal den of iniquity. One February morning at 1.a.m. an undercover team of four policemen and one woman were admitted into the house. Here they socialised with the guests who included two American officers and a number of 'fast' women. They paid £3 - roughly a week's wages - for a meal and drinks in the well-furnished rooms.

The illegal club was raided and the type of fancy fare only dreamed about by most Mancunians was discovered heaped high in the ample larder. Tratalos was fined £60 with £20 costs. His lawyer claimed he only set up the illegal catering and entertainment business so his children could go to good schools. There was much discussion in the newspapers about the cost of the police operation as they had run up bills, completely in the line of duty of course, totalling some £38 in hotel expenses. The high living had been necessary, they argued, so that they might get an invite to the illegal club. There had been no shortage of volunteers for this particular operation.

The casual younger female 'workers' aged between 13 and 17 years old were known as 'gadabout girls'. In summertime they often made their way to Blackpool and would spend the night on a tram. Without a father at home, and with mothers fatigued by war work, the girls were far less supervised than their elder sisters had been. They sought out and often had 'a good time' but the pleasure came with a price. In August, 1943, eight of the thirteen girls who appeared before Manchester juvenile court were suffering from venereal disease and four out of five girls admitted to a maternity home were under fifteen.

When discovered in the docks area at 1.30 a.m, Kathleen, 18, and Jessie, 20, were unable to produce identity cards. They were found with 'foreign seamen' and admitted to frequenting the area every night. Neither had had a day job for months and both were put on probation with the proviso that they undertook normal employment. Any more foreign semen and they would be off to Strangeways.

In Salford, Joan, an attractive 19-year-old, discharged from the ATS, was found to be suffering from a disease contracted whilst having a 'good time' as an absentee. Her father issued an ultimatum demanding that she must have medical treatment or leave the family home. Joan chose the second course of action and made off with her dad's watch and chain which she later pawned. Arrested and placed on trial, the teenager promised to behave herself and seek medical assistance. She was put on probation for twelve months.

82. The black-out at least enabled some men to live out their fantasies. This 39-year-old defence worker wandered the streets in the 1940's equivalent of drag. Though even in the dark conditions one would need to be extremely short-sighted to make a mistake over the gender of the night walker.

83. Tried in 1942, he was sentenced to a rather harsh eighteen months for gross indecency.

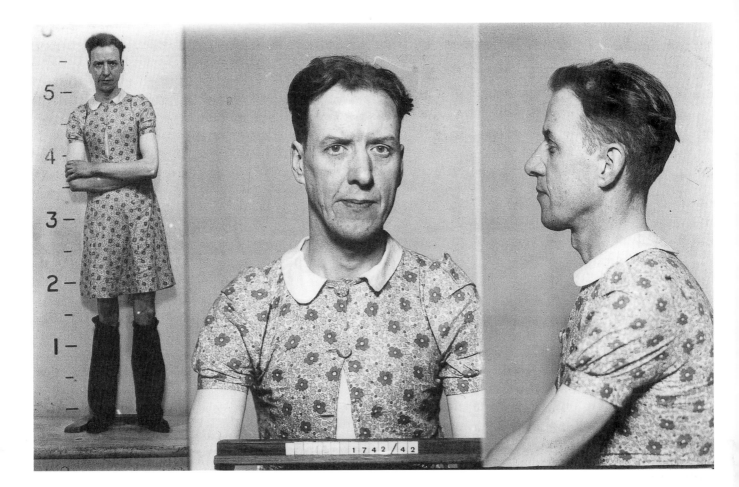

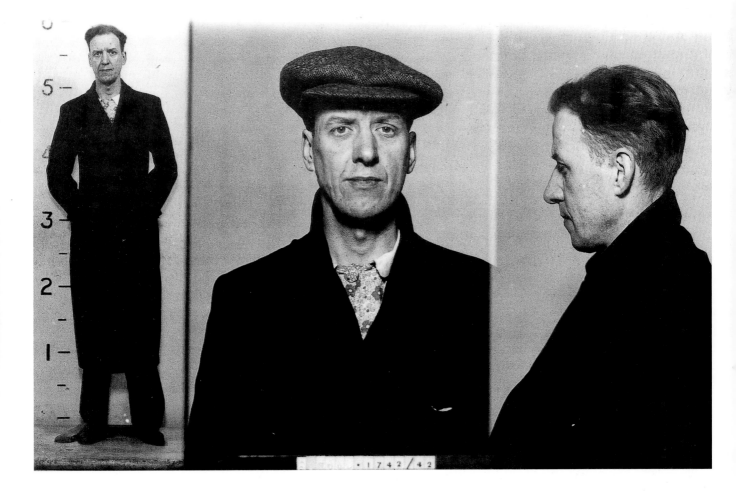

BRITISH BOBBIES VS. THE U.S.NAVY

Many foreign seamen determined to make their own entertainment. The following extract is from the Chief Constable of Salford's annual report for 1943:

"I have to report that during the evening of the 26th October, 1943, a number of American naval ratings and seamen entered the Cattle Market Hotel, Cross Lane, Salford. One of their number had been engaged in an altercation in the hotel on the previous night, during which he had received a head injury, and it was very soon apparent that they intended to create trouble.

They went into the dance room and at once commenced to interfere with the persons who were dancing. When a civilian remonstrated with them, he was immediately struck on the forehead and sustained a cut wound. Events followed with quick rapidity, and about 9.50. p.m. Superintendent Cleminson entered the room with six other officers. There was an immediate signal amongst a group of about 20/25 American sailors to resist the arrest of their compatriot who had wounded the civilian referred to above, and a fierce struggle ensued in which the Americans resorted to the use of any missile upon which they could lay their hands. Chairs were wielded and thrown about, whilst glasses and bottles were hurled by them in all directions.

The police were outnumbered but several civilians and members of H.M. Forces - about six in all - came to their assistance. It was not possible to identify individual acts on the part of the civilians as the fighting was taking place in various parts of the room and combatants were frequently changing. Finally the disturbance was quelled and ten naval ratings and three seamen were arrested."

The offenders would have been dealt with in their own court. Awards of about a week's wages were handed out to those assisting the police.

Rumours of an anti-American nature would spread very quickly and many Mancunians needed little excuse to pick a fight with their 'guests'. The Americans for their part were not averse to mixing it and would often trade insults - and blows - with their 'hosts'.

One totally false rumour just prior to the D-Day landings in June 1944 almost led to a full scale riot in Salford. Two local teenagers were ejected from a club in New Eccles road and apprehended when they tried to force their way back in. The sister of one of the arrested youths, who was still inside the hall, became hysterical, and, along with several girlfriends, began screaming, shouting and stomping. Police reinforcements were urgently summoned as a totally felonious rumour spread like wildfire throughout the hall and surrounding streets. A mob of over one thousand, most either tipsy or intoxicated, were looking for blood.

The story went that an American seaman had made an indecent suggestion to the hysterical sister in the dance hall. Whilst defending her honour, her brother had been arrested, batoned by the police and frogmarched through the streets while the American was allowed to go free.

As the two drunken young men were being loaded into the police van a large crowd surged forward in an attempt to rescue the 'wronged' brother. Another three drunkards were arrested and manhandled into the van.

With tempers flaring on both sides it needed a man of the cloth, respected by both parties, to help defuse a very volatile situation. Enter Alfred Wasey, the Rector of Stowell Memorial Church. Having personally verified the police account of events, he mingled with the potential rioters giving his word as a man of God that the young men arrested had not been brutally assaulted. He also insisted that the rumours about the American insults were false.

By 12.15. a.m. the crowd had gradually dispersed. The danger of a full-scale riot had been so serious that officials had contemplated calling out the Home Guard. The prisoners appeared in court the following morning. One young man was sent to prison for fourteen days on a charge of common assault and four others fined.

Tensions were not solely between the locals and American servicemen. The yanks seemed hell-bent on re-enacting their civil war on English soil. The bad blood between black and white, stationed in segregated camps, resulted in several skirmishes breaking out on the streets of Manchester and Salford. The British bobby had to take on a new role as sheriff.

The Chief Constable of Salford reported on a typical altercation in December. 1943:

"At 10.30.p.m. on Wednesday, the !st instant, Sergeant Blease and Constable 216 Ford observed two coloured American soldiers, Privates Frederick Davies (22 years) and George Booker (21 years), who were stationed at the Castle Irwell Racecourse, Salford, behaving in a disorderly manner in Eccles New Road, Salford, near to the Ship Hotel. Both men were drunk and were wielding short iron bars in each hand - parts of a cellar grating which they forcibly removed from the Grove Hotel about 40 yards away.

The two soldiers repeatedly expressed their intention of finding some American Marines with whom they had had an altercation the previous night. They refused to surrender the iron bars and all efforts to reason with them proved of no avail. The men were taken across Eccles New Road but when near to the Police Box at the corner of Trafford Road they commenced to fight and resist arrest.

The constable was struck several times about the hands and body with one of the iron bars and whilst the officers were struggling a civilian named Frank

84. The Chief Constable of Salford, Godfrey with Herbert Morrison and a rather important visitor inspecting the men who had to intervene in the disputes between American servicemen and locals (1941)

Harding (33) of 101, Stowell Street, Pendleton came to their assistance. The soldiers continued to struggle until three other police officers came on the scene and it took the combined efforts of the five police officers and Harding to get the men into the police box."

Harding was rewarded with a week's extra wages from the civic purse. Not all citizens were so eager to join an affray.

READ HITLER TALES FROM THE BIBLE

In the Manchester Conscientious Objectors tribunal of 1940 John Worthington was asked by the chairman what he would do if Hitler came to England to do what he had done in Poland. Worthington replied that he would read tales from the Bible to him. If Hitler was told where he was wrong he would listen carefully. John failed in his appeal (to the tribunal).

In April 1940, following the rejection of his appeal to be considered a conscientious objector, a supposed Mancunian pacifist followed the judge to the local railway station and stabbed him with a dagger as he was entering a compartment. It appears that the board's findings had been correct. The judge recovered and the offending objector spent the war years in prison for attempted murder.

Private Donald Adams was sentenced to one year's detention for disobeying, on nine occasions, an order to parade at Aldershot detention barracks. He was seen reading a Bible when he should have been preparing for the commandant's parade. Adams told the court that he was not wilfully defiant but 'could not control his other self'.

In 1943 Ernest Chenery appealed against sentence of one month's imprisonment for failing to comply with his national service order. A doctor testified that he would only rarely go out with his wife to the cinema as he had a morbid fear of being in a building with other people. He could not travel by train for the same reason and suffered from both claustrophobia and acrophobia. A frustrated chairman resignedly gave up the chase:

'He has a dread of being anywhere then?'

A MELANCHOLY BABY

Deserters would often be sheltered by family and friends who themselves risked prosecution. In 1943, looking for a man who had gone AWOL, the police visited Teresa Oakley's Manchester home on six different occasions. When she answered the door to greet her visitors Teresa would burst into song, each time offering a loud rendition of 'Melancholy Baby'. She continued in full voice as the house was searched "Cuddle up and don't be blue" etc. When asked whether this might be some kind of warning so a deserter may make good his escape or pop into a hiding hole, Teresa was insistent that she was only singing her favourite tune. Although no deserter was apprehended the song-bird was fined nine shillings. Teresa probably consoled herself with song. "Every cloud must have a silver lining."

85. McEwan, a Canadian deserter, was hanged for the murder of a retired postman. It was unlikely he would have faced the death penalty if he had been born South of the border.

Some deserters were fleeing more than a return to active duty. When seeking lodgings with a Mrs Annie Perfect in Cecil street, Chorlton-on-Medlock 'Jim Acton' posed as a merchant seaman who had been torpedoed and discharged for some time. In the summer of 1943, following a tip-off, police raided the house at 3 a.m. and questioned the man they found in bed. He was not the deserter they had targeted, but appeared very agitated. One of the policemen noticed part of a wing of an aeroplane tattooed on the man's arm, and, pulling back the bedclothes, revealed the full image of a plane in flight. The policeman had remembered his briefings and knew this to be one of the distinguishing marks of 35-year-old Mervin Clare McEwen, wanted in connection with the murder of an 83-year-old retired postman in Halifax. Being a commonwealth soldier and not American, McEwen was tried in a British court and executed at Armley Gaol, Leeds.

PLAYING COWBOYS AND INDIANS

The authorities also faced problems from those who did want to fight but were refused by the Army. To be rejected by the services one had to be medically unfit or extremely slow. Ernest Dobson, from Rusholme, wasn't medically unfit.

Along with his 17-year-old brother Wilfred, Ernest (20) held up a newspaper shop in Mauldeth Road. They only had one mask between them but continued with the raid regardless: Let's leave Ernest to take up the story in his own words:

" I had the cosh and I put a mask over my face. We went in the shop and pointed the cosh at the girl as if it was a pistol.

I said 'Put 'em up' and the girl went very red. She said 'Don't be silly' and when she turned to go into the back room we were frightened and ran away.

When I have to go in the Army I want to be a soldier not in the blinking Army Medical Corps. I want to be tough. That's why I did all this with my brother, they would not have me in the Army and I got fed up."

Wilfred added in a written statement:

"I want to join the Army too, but they won't have me... I hope I can get in the Amy now, I am tough."

Asked if they had any questions to ask the girl who had frightened them off by going into the back room Ernest, the elder of the tough brothers commented:

"We were only playing cowboys and Indians, that is all."

Detective-Inspector Timpany knew the Robson family well and told the court:

"Whenever I go to the house there always seems to be an addition to the family and these boys cannot say how many there are in the family, whether there are 12 or 13."

Somehow the war was won without the assistance of the Robson boys.

BAD, SAD OR MAD?

A certain understanding was shown by the court to those whose war experiences completely changed their character. Found wandering the streets with 30lbs of lead stolen from an empty house, 23-year-old John Owen was sympathetically treated by the arresting officer who asked the bench if something could be done for him. Owen had been evacuated from Dunkirk, had fought in Egypt and been blown up in Crete. Having been discharged from hospital, he was not wanted back by the army and was obviously suffering from shell-shock. He was remanded on bail and the first steps taken in the long journey to recovery were instigated.

Domestic murders continued throughout the hostilities. 73-year-old Cuthbert Waring strangled his wife Mary, 74, with a scarf at their home in Heywood road, Prestwick in September 1941. It was a typical case where small grievances had built up over the years and one party finally cracked. Their daughter told the court:

"On the whole they lived amicably but sometimes they disagreed about things. Sometimes mother thought father should stay in the house and help her in the morning instead of taking the dog out for a walk. There was at times some little feeling about the dog."

87. At least he had an original answer to the oft-asked question: 'what did you do in the war daddy?'

Cuthbert was found guilty but insane and ordered to be kept as a criminal lunatic until His Majesty's pleasure be known. The same sentence was passed on 37-year-old John Evans who strangled his mother with a tea-towel in the Autumn of 1943 in Wireworks Street, Moston. The 66-year-old widow and her labourer son displayed a strong affection for each other and there was no rational reason for the crime. John approached two reserve constables in St. Mary's road and later confessed to Detective Constable Liddy:

"I did it. I do not know what came over me. I did it with my hands. I have had fits of madness lately."

DISOBEYING THE SEVENTH COMMANDMENT

Despite her displaying obvious signs of paranoia, the senior medical officer at Strangeways considered Ruth Donnelly was fit to plead and responsible for her actions. The 62-year-old teacher believed that the Rector of St. Mary's Church in Hulme had been persecuting her after he gave evidence about her adultery which led to the successful divorce proceedings brought by her husband.

86. You never knew who you might bump into. The unknown warrior found wandering the streets of Manchester during air-raids.

The Reverend Walter Sydney Robinson was bombarded with malicious mail as part of a violent campaign against the man she believed had ruined her life. When he merely turned the other cheek the tormented teacher resolved that vengeance would be hers. Having been led into temptation she was now determined to deliver some evil. Dogging her quarry, Ruth slipped into the seat behind the man of God on a bus from Hulme to the city centre. Producing a small dagger she plunged it twice into the back of the neck of her prey. The clergyman was protected from what would have been more serious injuries by his collar. He turned to confront his attacker and sustained further injuries to his hands as he sought to protect himself from the flailing blows of a hysterical assailant.

When arrested the dagger wielder told Det. Inspector Timpany:

"It all started in the divorce court in 1940. I couldn't stand his diabolical laughter."

Defending counsel pleaded in mitigation that some time before, when Ruth Donnelly broke down while giving evidence in the divorce court, the rector was stated to have laughed. When the conductoress was collecting the fares he was said to have laughed again.

Ruth was sent down for two months.

In November, 1942, Edith Labrun was charged at Altrincham Police court with riotous behaviour at the spiritualist church. With eyes tight shut and arms outstretched, gesticulating and muttering, she sank against the witness box.

When asked how she pleaded she replied in a guttural voice:

"This is for you to find out, surely. I don't plead anything. You cannot decide this at a moment..... My guides appear. They take me everywhere and though you give me the direst penalty you cannot check that which I have done. You have heard your Prime Minister give you a doleful speech. I give you joy for ever."

Edith then commenced a long, loud barely comprehensible diatribe and was led from the courtroom. When summoned later, embarrassed court officials, possibly to everyone's relief, told the bench that Edith Labrun had disappeared.

BODY PUSHED THROUGH PORTHOLE

"I want you to arrest me for murder. I have murdered a man a long way off in Algiers. I strangled an Irishman in Algiers on June 21. He was named George Moore. It has been preying on my mind and I wish to tell you all about it."

George Anthony Cole, a 21-year-old merchant seaman from Riverside Avenue, Chorlton-cum-Hardy, a devout Roman Catholic, made his confession to an astonished policeman at the desk in Platt Lane Police station. Promptly arrested, Cole was tried at Manchester Assizes for the murder of an Irishman on a Belgian boat in Algiers. He pleaded not guilty to murder but did admit the killing. Let's hear some of his testimony:

"Religion has been playing on my mind. As you know, according to the Roman Catholic faith, if you take the Host in a state of sin it is sacrilege. I am accustomed to attending mass whenever I can, but I have lapsed it for some time. We have confession in my religion and if I confessed sin my religion states that I must give myself up to the law before that sin is forgiven.

Moore and I had a lot of trouble about religion. It was a case of the old Irish and English arguments cropping up. In addition to the repeated complaints I made about his dirty habits. He refused to use soap and water, and never changed his clothing.

On this particular night I had a few drinks, went to an E.N.S.A. show and finished by drinking Algerian wine, which takes the same effect as whisky after two hours...

When I asked him to undress he became noisy and quarrelsome. There were words and blows. As I got out of my bunk Moore struck me with a chair, hitting me on the head. When I came back to normal I saw Moore lying on the floor. I felt his pulse and found that he was dead. I saw the rope round his neck. I was nervous and agitated, and would not say that I was in my right mind."

The prosecution argued that Cole deliberately strangled his 16-year-old shipmate and forced the body through the porthole into the sea. The trussed up body was washed ashore. A rope had been tied tightly round the neck and body.

The jury were out for just twenty minutes. With two possible verdicts to consider - murder or manslaughter - they opted for the less serious charge. Mr Justice Lynskey did not appear to agree with their verdict. He told Cole:

"I think the jury have taken a very merciful view of this case. What you did was very near murder - if not murder."

He then passed a stiff sentence of ten years imprisonment. Cole, who in May 1941 had survived six days in an open boat and lost two toes to frostbite, was distraught. All colour drained from his cheeks as he colapsed in the dock and had to be carried to be his cell by a number of wardens.

"YOU HAVE CONDEMNED AN INNOCENT MAN"

88. The whole face of Manchester was transformed by the bombing and wartime emergency regulations.

The murder of Olive Balchin by Walter Rowland in October 1946 was, on the face of it, a fairly routine case of punter attacking prostitute, call girl and client falling out. It was not to prove so for two reasons: Rowland vehemently protested his innocence to the very end, and, another man, David John Ware, owned up to the crime. A few years later Ware proved beyond all doubt that he was capable of having carried it out. The facts are as follows.

Deansgate, one of Manchester's main thoroughfares, had suffered several direct hits during the bombing raids and bombsites were still awaiting clearance. More than one year after the end of hostilities broken bricks, splintered wooden beams and twisted pipes smothered in dust were a constant reminder of the futility of war. Rationing was, if anything, stricter than during the conflict. The first grapefruit seen in any numbers in Manchester for years were promised for November and a special allocation of bananas for the city's young people under 18 was eagerly awaited.

Prostitutes had made a good living during the war.

Sex was not on ration and with members from all branches of the armed services seeking relief, there was no shortage of demand for sexual favours. The laws of demand and supply, and the wealth of American servicemen, led to the more prudent prostitutes building up a tidy nest-egg.

By the Autumn of 1946 most men had returned to the bosom of their own homes and prices fell. The going rate for a 40-year-old blonde, greying at the temples, was ten shillings and supper. Customers, no longer raw young servicemen away from home for the first time, tended to be misfits and loners - solitary, sometimes dangerous men with quick tempers who drifted from casual job to no job and from lodging house to doss house.

Olive Balchin, a prostitute, and Walter Rowland, a drifter with a short fuse, got to know each other, in the Biblical sense, in August 1946. They had sex twice, once in the ruins of a bombed out building. He called her 'Lil' and she soon became one of his casual acquaintances, his 'friend' when in funds. About the same age, the pair most likely never spoke about their backgrounds. Olive had very low self-esteem, probably through never having been loved by her natural parents. Rowland had a much darker secret.

Who knows what drove a woman brought up in the atmosphere of a vicarage to do tricks with strangers for ten shillings? Olive moved to Manchester from Birmingham where she had worked as a maid for a Major. She answered to the name of Lily Wise but quickly tired of the skivvying job and, much to the consternation of her adopted family, all devout Christians, Olive a.k.a. Lily became a 'fallen woman' a Jezebel. A letter from her missionary foster brother, found in her handbag, implored her to return home and give up her way of life. Olive ignored all pleas and took up her own missionary position.

Before her murder, on the night of 19th October 1946, Olive had been earning a living on and off in Manchester for about nine months. She spent the last two months of her life in the Manchester Women's Hostel in Ashton House, Corporation street. Here she paid 10d. per night and was awoken at 8.a.m. but rarely left before midday. Olive kept herself to herself and never dined with the other residents. One of two fellow lodgers who knew her vaguely later told the police:

'She never mixed with anyone here, she appeared to have a good upbringing.. I was particularly struck by the sad pale face. Her thoughts always seemed to be so far away.'

Walter Rowland was born in 1908, the same year as Olive. Not having experienced the trauma of adoption, he appeared to get on well with his parents. Of above average intelligence, Rowland served an apprenticeship as an engineer before joining the Army as an 18-year-old. Detesting the discipline, he begged his parents to purchase his discharge which they duly did just two months later. Lacking self-discipline, and with the brashness of youth, he was sacked from the ensuing labouring job for insolence. A second flirtation with the services resulted in his discharge after just two weeks when the Royal Tank Corps found him medically unfit.

He now started to show signs of being psychologically 'unfit'. In 1927 the sacked soldier first displayed a cruel streak of violence he later had no hesitation in employing - at least against women and children. Rowland tried to strangle a young woman named May Schofield and was sentenced to three years at the academy of crime - Borstal. Here he made his first attempt at suicide when unsuccessfully trying to hang himself. Released on licence, Rowland returned to labouring and married, his wife dying later that year during childbirth. The following year Rowland remarried, Annie May Schofield - almost certainly the same young woman he had tried to strangle four years previously. The couple had a love/hate relationship. The love resulted in the birth of a baby daughter in 1932. The hate was viciously displayed two years later when Rowland strangled to death the defenceless young girl he had fathered.

Rowland was a man who seemed to hate himself. He made two further attempts at ending his own life by drinking Lysol and iodine, but it appeared the state would be willing to carry out his wishes at the taxpayer's expense. Following his wife's testimony against him, Rowland was sentenced to be hanged.

Eight years later in 1942, the malicious misfit was free again. The strangler had been reprieved and was sent off to war to take lives, this time with the full approval of the state. In June 1946, Rowland left the Army. Still unable to control his temper, he had attempted to strike a sergeant while in uniform. Walter Rowland slunk back to his parent's home and spent most of his time in Manchester, drifting and living on the proceeds of crime. He was known to consort with prostitutes and enjoyed 'kicking them about'.

On the night of Saturday, 19th October, a man and woman were seen in heated argument at the corner of Deansgate and Cumberland Street. Despite the late hour the licensee of the Dog and Partridge got a good look at the feuding couple but dismissed the altercation as a lovers' tiff.

Shortly before midday the following morning, some children playing in the ruins of the nearby bombsite, stumbled across a body far too fresh to

89. Death in Deansgate. The body of 40-year-old Olive Balchin.

have been a casualty of war. The corpse was that of a thin woman about 40 years old. She was fully dressed in a navy blue costume, half belted overcoat with large pearl buttons, black shoes size 6 and lisle stockings. On her marriage finger she wore a signet ring. Few witnesses took note of the apparel at the time, the focus of attention being the woman's head that had been smashed with such force that the brain was protruding. Copious amounts of blood stained the head and surrounding debris and must have soaked the clothes of her assailant. Lying beside her was a hammer, later confirmed as the murder weapon. This was no ordinary hammer however, as the police would later discover. In the handbag were two identity cards, one in the name of 'Olive Balchin' and the other 'Lily Wise' both with different addresses in Birmingham. A ten shilling note and some change were discovered in the purse. Robbery was not the motive.

Tracing the murderer of a prostitute is often complicated due to the reluctance of regular clients to come forward. Finding the murderer of a woman comparatively new on the block would be very tricky indeed.

The best lead was the murder weapon whose details and photograph were released to the local press. Detectives were delighted at the rapid response from a Mr. Edward MacDonald who ran a broker's shop in Ardwick. He had bought the hammer on the morning of 19th October and sold it

again that evening. He particularly remembered the sale because the tool was of the type used by leather-dressers and not suitable for general purposes. He warned the customer, who seemed indifferent, and left with his purchase in a paper bag.

Meanwhile the licensee who had seen a couple quarrelling phoned the police to tell them of the altercation he had witnessed near the site where the body was found. He was driven to the mortuary, and, despite the 'sorry state' of the victim, identified her as the woman he'd noticed in the heated dispute. Both the licensee and the vendor of the hammer gave a description of the man they had seen:

DESCRIPTION BY	LICENSEE	VENDOR
AGE	30-35	28-32
HEIGHT	5' 7"	5' 7" - 5' 8"
BUILD	proportionate	medium
CLOTHES	blue suit	dark suit, fawn raincoat
APPEARANCE	clean shaven	clean shaven
	clean and tidy	clean and respectable
HAIR	dark	dark

90. Walter Graham Rowland, one of the few men to have been sentenced to hang on two separate occasions. He still has his supporters today who believe in his innocence.

A third witness, a waitress in a cafe off Deansgate, told police that a woman she identified as Olive, a man, with dark hair and a dark suit, and another woman were in the cafe between 10.30 and 11. 30 on the night of the murder. The trail was hot. So far the investigators had the following timetable of events for 19th October.

5.30.p.m.: man buys hammer, later confirmed as the murder weapon.

10.30.p.m.: man with similar appearance spends one hour in a cafe off Deansgate with Olive and another woman.

12.p.m.: Olive and man with same description seen quarrelling near where the body is later discovered.

Detectives had a reasonable description of their suspect but so far no motive. Most murders of prostitutes were effected in the heat of the moment. The man who killed Olive had bought the murder weapon several hours previously. This crime was premeditated, but why and by whom?

The police set out on the dogged leg-work essential in a case of this kind. Each officer was allotted lodging-houses and hostels and told to question the transient population responsible for so many of the crime statistics. As with a large number of cases, the police stumbled upon the name of the man they finally arrested by chance. One of the many interviewees stated that he had lent his raincoat to a man named Roland and it had not been returned. A swift check of the criminal records showed that Rowland, with a 'W', matched the description and was known as a violent man.

Six days after the murder, John Rowland was traced to the Services Transit dormitory where he was rousted from his bed at 11. p.m. and asked to accompany the policemen to the station. Later in court there was a difference of opinion as to what was said at the time of arrest, the police arguing that Rowland implicated himself which he vehemently denied.

He did not, however, deny knowing Olive and admitted that he had been with her the day before the sighting in the cafe, on 18th October. He sought her out to ask her if she was responsible for passing on a venereal disease which he had recently had diagnosed. Rowland professed to being proud of his body and was extremely angry about the infection. Although he denied murdering Olive, he did foolishly state that if she had given him V.D. 'she deserved all that she got.'

At last the police had their motive.

At two subsequent identity parades Rowland was picked out by the vendor of the hammer, the cafe worker and the licensee. Things were not looking too good for the drifter who continually changed his alibi for the night of the murder. He finally stuck with his being in lodgings at 81, Brunswick street. The registration book, however, showed him as leaving on the 19th. In Rowland's defence the landlord argued that the date should have read the 20th.

The trial opened on December 12th, 1946, and lasted four days. One juror was excused because he did not believe in capital punishment.

The case against Rowland looked very strong. He knew the victim; he had a motive; he had no watertight alibi and he had been identified by three witnesses. Forensics showed that brick-dust, cement, charcoal, clinker and withered tissue from the building site were found in the turn-ups of his trousers. On his left shoe was a stain of human blood.

The defence had little alternative but to clutch at straws.

In an assault as vicious as that upon Olive, the attacker's clothes, they argued, would normally have been expected to be soaked in the blood of the victim. There was not one trace of blood found upon the arrested man's clothes. His fingerprints were not on the hammer or wrapping paper and serious doubts about identification were surfacing. One main concern was that Rowland did not have dark hair as the witnesses suggested and he argued that he never used hair cream which may have created a dark effect.

On Monday, 16th December at 6.35.p.m., after

deliberating just under two hours the jury returned a verdict of 'guilty'. Some may have questioned their judgment when over the next few minutes Rowland first replied:

"May God forgive you. You have condemned an innocent man."

When asked if he had anything else to say why sentence of death should not be passed, Walter Rowland, without the assistance of notes, made the following impassioned speech from the dock:

"Yes, I have, my Lord. I have never been a religious man, but as I have sat in this court during these last few hours the teachings of my boyhood have come back to me, and I say in all sincerity and before you and this Court that when I stand in the Court of Courts before the Judge of Judges I shall be acquitted of this crime. Somewhere there is a person who knows that I stand here today an innocent man. The killing of this woman was a terrible crime, but there is a worse crime been committed now, my Lord, because someone with the knowledge of this crime is seeing me sentenced today for a crime which I did not commit. I have a firm belief that one day it will be proved in God's own time that I am totally innocent of this charge, and the day will come when this case will be quoted in the Courts of this country to show what can happen to a man in a case of mistaken identity. I am going to face what lies before me with the fortitude and calm that only a clear conscience can give. That is all I have to say, my Lord."

Mr. Justice Sellars then condemned Walter Rowland to death. He became one of a very small handful to hear this sentence twice.

On the weight of evidence the verdict seems to be correct. The sorry story would be forgotten today had their not been a new bizarre development in January, 1947. With Rowland ticking off his remaining days on the calendar, news filtered through to him that another man had confessed to the murder and was 'singing' in Liverpool gaol. No self-respecting fiction writer would introduce a new character so late in the plot. Enter David John Ware in the final chapter of the tragic tale. An edited version of his confession read:

"I bought a hammer after some searching near the railway station...At 6.p.m. I met Olive Balchin outside the Hippodrome. I spoke to her and suggested going to the pictures...[Later that evening] The spot where we stopped was a place or building that I took to be bombed in the war. We went inside the ruins and stood for a short while near the entrance.

91. David John Ware who confessed to the murder of Olive Balchin. He showed years later that he was perfectly capable of having carried out such a crime.

We were quite close to each other and being so near she took the opportunity of going through my pockets. I was aware of this but did not show her. I was ate up with hatred and felt immediately I'd like to kill her...I struck her a violent blow on the head (I should say the right side). She screamed and before her scream lasted any length of time I struck her again, this time she only mumbled. Her hands were on her head protecting it the second time she fell to the floor up against the wall and I repeated the blows. Blood shot up in a thin spray. I felt it on my face and then I panicked and threw the hammer and left everything as it was."

Ware stated that he spent the rest of the night in a lodging house in Stockport, tramped to Buxton and hitched a lift to Sheffield where he owned up to a robbery from a Salvation Army hostel in Stoke. He had been in custody ever since. The police were used to bogus confessions but nonetheless had to check each one out.

To do so they needed to know a little more about the man who was putting his hands up to murder.

Born in the same year as Walter Rowland, Ware embarked on an unsuccessful career of petty crime at an early age. His first term of bird -12 months - was in 1931, following a pathetic attempt at blackmail. Like Rowland, Ware married, but chose to abandon his family rather than strangle them. Once again, like Rowland, he joined the army in 1942 but only served one year before being discharged suffering from manic-depressive psychosis. The rest of the war he spent in and out of gaol for minor offences.

Both Rowland and his solicitors must have been encouraged by the unexpected turn of events. Here was a man owning up to the crime Rowland had persistently denied. On January 27th, Rowland's appeal was adjourned for fourteen days. On February 10th, his application for Ware to give evidence was refused and his appeal dismissed. However, with the uncertainty caused by the confession, the authorities, wanted to be certain they were going to execute the right man. It's a tragedy they were not so vigilant in the later cases of Evans and Hanratty. The home secretary ordered a king's counsellor, a Mr. Jolly, to conduct an enquiry into Ware's confession.

The three identity witnesses were recalled and none could pick Ware out from an identity parade. When subsequently confronted with Ware in a one-to-one, replies of 'nothing like him' and 'definitely not' were elicited. Mr. Jolly found so many anomalies and inconsistencies in Ware's story that the confession was withdrawn on 22nd February.

Prisoner John Ware, no 7305, began his withdrawal:

"I wish to say that statements I have been confessing to a murder are totally untrue. I have never seen the woman Balchin, who was murdered in Manchester, in my life."

Rowland was hanged on February 27th 1947.

For the record no trace of any venereal disease was discovered on the body of Olive Balchin.

Four years later David John Ware, now living in Bristol, entered a hardware shop and purchased a hammer. He went to the Downs and struck up a conversation with a woman. She accepted his invitation to go for a walk. As they were about to sit down on the grass, Ware produced the hammer and struck his victim a meaty blow on the skull. Fortunately, with the force of the contact, the head of the hammer flew off and Ware could only continue his assault with the shaft. He quickly abandoned the attack and fled. He turned himself in three days later.

At the subsequent trial for attempted murder Ware was found guilty but insane and sent to Broadmoor. Three years later, on All Fools day, Ware hanged himself.

ILLUSTRATION ACKNOWLEDGEMENTS

THE IMPERIAL WAR MUSEUM:
2, 3, 6, 9,12,13,19a,19b,25,25a,30,42,46,49,67,72.

POPPERFOTO:
7,8,10,11,14,15,16,18,27,29,31,39,45,47,50,51,55, 61,63,65,69,70

HULTON DEUTSCH:
24,26,28,34,35,40,52,59,64,71,73

TOPHAM PICTURE SOURCE:
17,32,41,43,44,48,53,54,57,60,62,66,74

GREATER LONDON RECORD OFFICE:
1,4,5,56,58,68

TOWER HAMLETS LIBRARY:
5,37,58,77

PUBLIC RECORD OFFICE:
20,21,22,23,33,36,75,76,78

AFTER THE BATTLE (No 45)
38.

MANCHESTER POLICE MUSEUM:
79,80,81,82,83,84,86,87,89,90,91

ACKNOWLEDGEMENTS

I would very much like to thank Duncan and Chris at the Manchester Police Museum, Viv Foster my editor, and Steve Arnold. Their avice, professionalism and attention to detail helped me retain my sanity when the going got tough.

Wicked Publications

STEVE JONES

After having worked in France, Denmark, The United States, Australia, Yorkshire, Derbyshire, London and Nottinghamshire, I have left teaching Modern Languages to start another career.

My full time job now involves researching writing and collecting photographs for our publications.

After being offered a miserly 6% by an established publisher for the first book, I decided to go it alone and have all our publications privately printed which has helped keep costs down.

I believe there is a keen interest in both crime and history and a strong demand for the early photographs, detailed illustrations and relevant contemporary accounts.

If you enjoy our books please tell your friends or drop us a line.

Have a 'Wicked' read.

"I have had opportunities of witnessing, in rooms measuring not more than 14 feet square, from 15 to 20 men, women and children lodged, the men and children completely naked, with the exception of a small rug and the women with nothing more than a shift, which, from the length of time and the filthy habits of the wearer, had the appearance of oil cloth more than the undergarment of a female; they were all breathing an atmosphere pestilential in the extreme." Police superintendent Schorey, Gateshead, 1850.

I was blind at the time with passion, and I picked up a stone and hit her with it and she fell down in the same place where the body was picked up. Sunderland pitman James Burton's confession after the killing of his wife 1883.

Two contemporary accounts of life and crime in Northumberland and Old County Durham. With tales from Berwick to Darlington, petty-theft to mass-murder, join us in an uncensored trip back in time. Who knows, with details of hundreds of offenders and many photographs, you may just meet one of your ancestors.

Ellen Woodman (11) 7 days for stealing scrap metal. Newcastle, 1873.

Henry Stephenson (12) 2 months with solitary confinement for housebreaking. Newcastle, 1873.

Northumberland and Durham... The Sinister Side

ATTEMPTED MURDER AND SUICIDE AT GATESHEAD

Steve Jones   A Wicked Publication

All books are A4 with at least 80 photographs/illustrations to supplement the wicked tales of yesteryear.

**(1) London...
The Sinister Side**
Reprinted every year since 1986. Includes chapters on Jack the Ripper, The Kray Twins, executions, the hangmen of London, prisons. If you are interested in the darker side of London's history, its ghosts, murderers, mystery and misery, then join us in our trip through London.... The Sinister Side.

(2) Wicked London
Murder 'Orrible Murder, the Blitz, early operations and the darker side of everyday life.

(3) Through the Keyhole
Reveals secrets previously guarded behind locked doors, nineteenth century divorce cases, illicit love affairs, prostitution and night life

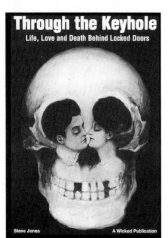

(4) Capital Punishment
These wicked tales of yesteryear are centred around the crime, domestic violence and prison conditions in Victorian London. Including sections on juvenile crime, dangerous woman, the lighter side of court life and women in prison.

(5) In Darkest London
Prostitutes, criminals, backstreet abortionists, strikers and the police give lengthy accounts of their activities in a frank and unsentimental look at London life from the death Victoria to the outbreak of the Second World War.

**(6) Birmingham...
The Sinister Side**
Pickpockets, petty thieves, prostitutes,drunks, murderers and wife beaters galore. The people in its pages, staring bac at the reader from police 'mug shots' with grim resignation, pathos or rebellion in their eye sandwiched between spine-chilling 'penny dreadful' illustrations portraying scenes red murder and callous brutali

**(7) Nottingham...
The Sinister Side**
Although internationally famous being the home of Britain's most famous outlaw, Robin Hood, Nottingham, like all large cities, h housed tens of thousands of lawbreakers with no intention whatsoever of giving to the poor. The most famous murderers inclu 'Nurse' Waddingham who poison two of her patients for their inheritance, and Herbert Mills, w executed 'the perfect murder' in order to sell his story to the newspapers - both were hanged.

**(8) Manchester...
The Sinister Side**
With the presence of over 100 photographs and illustrations, join us in a tri back in time to meet the incorrigible rogue's, vagabonds and thieves in Victorian Manchester and t atrocious conditions endure by the vast majority of the population.

Wicked Publications, 222 Highbury Road, Bulwell, Nottingham NG6 9FE
Tel/Fax: Nottingham (0115) 975 6828 or Tel: (020) 8311 3888